2012

Praise for Willie Nelson's
Roll Me Up and Smoke Me When I Die

"Nelson's unmistakable voice shines through . . . funny, inspirational and bawdy, with a well-honed sense of humor." —*Kirkus Reviews*

"An irreverent, entertaining read. Humble, optimistic, and quick to give credit to those around him for contributing to his success, Nelson is a charming narrator." —*Publishers Weekly*

"Nelson takes us for a rollicking ride along the highways and byways of his long life and career in this rambunctious, hilarious, reflective, and loving memoir." —*American Songwriter*

"Compelling page-turner . . . for all his fame and accessibility, he still has so much wisdom left to share." —Jambands.com

"Compact and breezy volume . . . laugh-out-loud funny. . . . For those who want to feel as if they're just shooting the shit with a friend—albeit a well-traveled and world famous one."
—*Houston Press*

"A Rabelaisian idyll, mixing contemporary journal entries with reminiscences from friends and family and plenty of profane good humor." —*Atlanta Journal-Constitution*

"So many decades into his fabled life and career, Willie fans pretty much know what to expect from him. And he does not let his readers down with his *Musings from the Road*."
—Country Music Television, Nashville Skyline blog

"Feels like Willie Nelson . . . and it effectively conveys the wildness of a long career in popular music. He's not working in his principal medium here, but Willie Nelson remembers the value of entertainment." —*Paste Magazine*

ALSO BY WILLIE NELSON

FICTION

A Tale Out of Luck

NONFICTION

The Tao of Willie: A Guide to the Happiness in Your Heart (with Turk Pipkin)

The Facts of Life and Other Dirty Jokes

Willie: An Autobiography (with Bud Shrake)

ROLL ME UP
AND
SMOKE
ME
WHEN I DIE

MUSINGS
FROM THE ROAD

WILLIE NELSON

FOREWORD BY KINKY FRIEDMAN
ILLUSTRATIONS BY MICAH NELSON

wm

WILLIAM MORROW
An Imprint of HarperCollins*Publishers*

A hardcover edition of this book was published in 2012 by William Morrow, an imprint of HarperCollins Publishers.

FIRST WILLIAM MORROW PAPERBACK EDITION PUBLISHED 2013.

Designed by Jamie Lynn Kerner

Library of Congress Cataloging-in-Publication Data has been applied for.

ISBN 978-0-06-229331-2

19 20 21 DIX!/LSC 10

To my mother and father, Myrle and Ira Nelson,
who blazed a musical trail for me
and Sister Bobbie to follow

WILLIE NELSON: THE FOREWORD

BY KINKY FRIEDMAN

In April 1933, Willie's mother, Myrle, gave birth to him in a manger somewhere along the old highway between Waco and Dallas. There were angels in attendance that night, and there would be for the rest of his life. Some of them, no doubt, flying too close to the ground.

In 1939, when Willie Nelson was six years old, he received his first real guitar. Hitler had just invaded Poland; the World's Fair had just opened in New York; and in Hollywood, *Gone with the Wind* had just beat out a quirky little film called *The Wizard of Oz* for Best Picture of the Year. These things were very probably not known to young Willie. Nor was he aware that his grandfather had just purchased a cheap Stella guitar from the Sears catalog. It would not be a cheap guitar to Willie; it would become his most prized possession, an instrument of transcendental beauty.

Unlike many famous people who left their hometowns and never looked back, Willie felt Abbott was always the home of his heart. It was where he was born, where Daddy and Mama Nelson raised him, and where he wrote his first poems and songs. He would come back many times to play concerts there, or maybe just dominoes; to visit old friends; and to reconnect with the land and the memories.

Willie's ticket out of Abbott was music, and to make it in music you had to be able to draw a crowd. The population of Abbott at the time Willie lived there, according to Bobbie, was a little over two hundred people. But, she added, you never could prove that. The little town simply could not hold all of Willie's dreams. Like the cat who always goes into the neighbor's garbage cans, he wanted to go to all the places where the music on his radio came from.

Once he left Abbott, Willie was traveling light like the gypsy in his soul. He'd been a songwriter since he was six years old; why the hell should he try to change course now? He kept writing songs and took gigs whenever and wherever he could get them; sometimes they fell like manna from the skies, sometimes they just seemed to dry up like a river in the drought. When he could, Willie found work as a country music disc jockey, playing some of the music that had influenced and inspired him throughout his childhood—Lefty Frizzell, Ernest Tubb, Hank Williams, Ray Price, Hank Snow, and, for sure, Bob Wills and the Texas Playboys.

MERLE HAGGARD ONCE REPORTEDLY SAID TO WILLIE, REGARDING Kris Kristofferson, the most talented janitor in Nashville, "You know, that guy is probably the best songwriter in town." Willie is said to have responded, "After you and me."

Willie, of course, a wordsmith since childhood, had already spent a lifetime pursuing his craft. Miss Dianne, Willie's first-grade teacher in Abbott, was one of the very earliest to notice his songwriting talent. She read some of his poems, soon to be lyrics, and was quite deeply impressed. She told Mama Nelson to keep an eye on this boy, because he was going to be something special. In Nashville, however, he found himself rapidly becoming the songwriter's songwriter. In other words, he was too hip for the room.

The word "songwriter" can apply to many different kinds of people. Barry Manilow is an accomplished songwriter and he's made more money than God. Basically, he writes songs that make you feel good for a short period of time. Willie, on the other hand, writes songs that may make you think, and some of them will stay with you for a lifetime.

Willie is hesitant about giving advice on songwriting. "I will never say anything to discourage a songwriter," he says. "But if you are a real songwriter, nothing I could say would discourage you, anyhow. If my opinion could change your mind about being a songwriter, then you really weren't a songwriter to begin with and I would have done you a favor by making you look for a different career. If a real songwriter happened to hear that I didn't like his work, he would say, 'What the hell does Willie Nelson know? Fuck Willie Nelson.'"

We come to see what we want to see in this world. The same song may have a totally different meaning to different people, and the guy who wrote it may have an entirely different interpretation from any of them. Willie says there is no formula for writing songs. You might add to that that there is also no formula for relating to songs or understanding them in any one particular way. In my opinion, "Kaw-Liga," the song about the wooden Indian who falls in love, is one of the saddest songs Hank Williams ever wrote. But I saw an old compilation of his work recently that some record company had put together long ago. The album was entitled *Kaw-Liga and Other Humorous Songs*. It's a close-to-the-heart, personal matter, and it's all in the ear of the beer-holder. Sometimes a writer's best work is what is written between the lines—in other words, what the song leaves up to the imagination of the listener. "If a song is true for you," Willie says, "it will be true for others."

In 1969, during the week before Christmas, Willie and Hank Cochran wrote a song that dealt not so subtly with the frustrations he was going through regarding his life and his career. The song was entitled "What Can You Do to Me Now?" A day or two later, on the night before Christmas Eve, Willie was in Nashville at a party when somebody came up to him and told him that the Ridgetop house had just burned down. Willie rushed home to find, much to his relief, that all of his extended family and all of his animal family were safe. But the house had been destroyed, along with almost everything he owned. He stumbled through the ashes until at last he found an old guitar case, inside of which were two pounds of Colombian tea. In the late sixties there were places you could get life in prison for getting caught with one joint.

Perhaps Willie took it as a sign. Perhaps, as he said, he was just feeling like "a minnow in a dipper." Whatever the reason, it was time to jump back in the river. When you write a song called "What Can You Do to Me Now?" and almost immediately afterward your house burns down, it would appear that somebody is trying to tell you something. If it was God speaking to Willie, She was only telling him what he'd already been thinking himself.

Willie is that rare bird who never bothers to sift the ashes after the fire has gone. He is forever embracing the future, even if it slaps him in the face. Most of the time it hugs him back. So he followed in the footsteps of another iconoclastic American hero who'd made the trek almost a hundred and fifty years earlier. Willie told the Nashville music establishment the same words Davy Crockett had told the Tennessee political establishment: "Y'all can go to hell— I'm going to Texas."

This move went deeper than the simple, obvious fact that Willie didn't fit in musically and stylistically with the Nashville Sound. The deeper problem was that in the sixties the good ol' boy network that was the music establishment was dead set against ever accepting Willie as one of them. They feared and despised his lifestyle—i.e., smoking pot. To the good ol' boy southern, Christian, straitlaced, humorless, constipated prigs who ran Music Row, dope was indubitably the devil. Country music, whatever its blessings and faults, would never gather reefer madness unto its collective, commercial, corporate bosom. That, indeed, was at the very heart of the problem. But it would not be a problem in Texas.

Like Davy Crockett before him, Willie would walk into history by way of his pilgrimage to Texas. Texas, where even before the music caught up with the ethos, outlaws were celebrated. But Willie did gain some practical wisdom from his Nashville experiences: "Get yourself a good Jewish lawyer before you sign anything, no matter how much the company says they love you."

Many years have come and gone, but the great body of work that Willie managed to create along with a small handful of others still resonates today, shining like musical diamonds in the rough despite the changing seasons, trends, and times. They were songwriters and they created some of their best work when they were broke, drunk, and stoned half the time. Maybe more than half.

Throughout his life, Willie has written most of his lyrics on scraps of paper, cocktail napkins, and worse. He wrote "Shotgun Willie" on a sanitary-napkin envelope. He wrote "On the Road Again" on a vomit bag. I once asked him whether he found it interesting that he wrote "On the Road Again," one of the greatest road anthems of all time, while on an airplane, and that he wrote "Bloody Mary Morning," a poignant portrayal of a heartbroken man on an airplane flight, while on the ground. He never really responded to my question. Of course, he was smoking a joint the size of a large kosher salami at the time.

This may indeed be conjuring up a romantic vision of Willie and the others, but when compared to today's Music Row, you can't help but see the obvious difference. Nashville after Willie and the boys is not the same. For decades now it seems to have spawned corporate publishing brothels, replete with long hallways filled with tiny little rooms each inhabited by two or three young songwriters who rushed to get to their songwriting appointment by four thirty sharp. In theory, this could produce some great new music; in practice, it has only resulted in the homogenized, sanitized, and derivative tissue of horseshit you usually hear on the radio these days.

Surely these writers are making money for somebody or the publishing corporations wouldn't be paying them. But it is worth mentioning that in the more than three decades since Willie got out of Dodge, nobody has written "Hello Walls." Nobody has written "Me and Bobby McGee." Nobody's written "Silver Wings." And nobody's written "King of the Road."

I asked Willie why he thought that was, and he didn't have a ready answer except to say that back then times were really tough. Perhaps that is the answer; perhaps this modern crop of songwriters, though not untalented, was merely born too late. Great art is rarely produced by someone who sits down to paint his masterpiece. The guy who sets out to write the great American novel never does it; the great work is invariably written by the guy who was just trying to pay the rent. Of course, it helps if you're a genius. But if you're a genius, you probably fucked up and missed your four-thirty songwriter's appointment.

ROLL ME UP
AND
SMOKE
ME
WHEN I DIE

EARLY MEMORIES

I'm flashing back to my first memories; they are of a blacksmith shop in Abbott, Texas. My grandfather is shoeing a horse. He is heating the horseshoe in the roaring hot coals in the furnace. I'm standing on my tiptoes turning the bellows that blows the air on the furnace, keeping the fire going. He heats the horseshoe till it is red-hot, then fits it to the horse's hoof, cools it off in water, and nails it onto the horse's hoof. A horse kicked him one day and ruptured his stomach.

He wore a truss the rest of his life until he died from pneumonia at fifty-six. I was seven years old at the time my grandfather died.

The next memory is my first introduction to gospel music. It is of a tabernacle that sat next to my house, where in the summertime we had revivals. The Methodists, the Baptists, and the Church of Christ all held their church services in the tabernacle. I am sitting at the table looking out the window, listening to them all. My first performance in church was when I was about five. I was wearing a white sailor suit with red trim. I start to recite a poem my grandmother taught me, but I have been picking my nose, which now starts to bleed. I hold my nose with one finger and while blood runs all over my little white sailor suit I recite my poem:

> *What are you looking at me for?*
> *I ain't got nothin' to say*
> *If you don't likes the looks of me*
> *Just look the other way*

My next memory is of our bumblebee fights. On Sundays we would all go out and fight bumblebees. I was ten years old. The farmers around Abbott would run into bumblebee nests during the week while they worked their fields. They would let us know where to go, and eight or ten of us boys would go out and fight the bees. Some days I would come home with both eyes swollen shut from bee stings.

What fun we had!

We made paddles, sawed out of wooden boxes, that looked like Ping-Pong paddles with holes. One of us would go in and shake the nest and stir up the bees. Then, when the bees were swarming, everyone would start swinging. The bees always headed for your eyes.

The next memory is when we (the same bee-hunting boys and me) are all hiding behind a billboard sign on the main road, Highway 81, that runs through Abbott, which is between Waco and Dallas. We have tied a string to a lady's purse that we laid in the middle of the highway. A car would come by, see the purse, hit the brakes, stop, and back up to get the purse. At that moment we would pull the purse back to us behind the billboard sign. The driver would then realize that it was a prank, give us the finger, and speed away. We laughed a lot.

Another great Sunday!

REDDY THE COW

Reddy was a big brown milk cow that I literally grew up on. Reddy was my first "horse." She was the first thing that I ever rode in my life, other than a stick horse. One of the first pictures that I ever saw of myself was of me sitting on Reddy's back. I couldn't have been more than two years old. I rode her all the time. It was my job, as I got older, to stake her out with a twenty-foot rope to graze on any grass I could find in Abbott. In the evening, I would

go pick her up and ride her back home to her barn. On the way home, she always wanted to run because she could smell the barn, and she knew she was going to get fed, have some water, and get great treatment. It was also my job to take her to a bull about a mile away, when she came in heat. She seemed to sort of pick up the pace on the way to the bull. I never seemed to have any trouble getting her to go over there—Reddy was always ready!—but she walked a little slower on the way back.

A BETTER WAY TO MAKE A BUCK

One day while I was picking cotton, on a farm by the highway that ran between Abbott and Hillsboro—it was about a hundred degrees in the hot Texas sun, and there I was pulling along a sack of cotton—a Cadillac came by with its windows rolled up. There was something about that scene that made me start thinking more about playing a guitar. Here I was picking cotton in the heat and thinking, There's a better way to make a dollar, and a *living,* than picking cotton. Sister Bobbie and I picked cotton on all the farms around Abbott every summer and every day after school. In Abbott, the schools let out at noon during harvest season, so we could all work in the fields. That's how we made our extra money. I did a lot more farmwork than Sister Bobbie, things like baling hay and working in the cotton gin and on the corn sheller, all of which was very hard work but in a lot of ways was good for me because it made me work harder on my guitar.

SISTER BOBBIE

Willie and I were born to Ira and Myrle Nelson in a small Texas town called Abbott. I was born in 1931 and Willie in 1933. Our parents were seventeen when I was born and nineteen years old at Willie's birth. We always lived with our grandparents, our father's parents. They had moved to Texas from Arkansas the year before I was born. Ira and Myrle were married in Arkansas at the age of sixteen in order for Myrle to come to Texas with Ira and his family. The marriage lasted only long enough for Willie and me to be born. We continued living with our grandparents William Alfred and Nancy Nelson. Our grandfather was a blacksmith. A large man in stature, a quiet man but very strong in spirit, Daddy Nelson never spoke unkindly of anyone. He was very protective of Willie and me. Our grandparents were students of music and studied the music that they received through mail-order courses by lamplight every night after supper. This was our inspiration and these were our teachers.

Our grandmother Mama Nelson was our music instructor. Daddy Nelson insisted that Mama start teaching us before we started school. We had a pump organ that I received my first music lessons on.

Daddy Nelson got sick with the flu and then pneumonia when I was nine and Willie was seven years old. He died only two weeks after he got sick. But before he died he had already bought a piano for me and a guitar for Willie. He made sure I learned to play the piano a little and he had already taught Willie some guitar. Daddy Nelson played stringed instruments, and Mama Nelson had knowledge of music from her father, who taught voice classes at singing schools in Arkansas. He traveled by horseback and buggy teaching singing classes. Our grandparents were gospel music singers. Daddy Nelson's voice was very beautiful; he was a tenor.

Willie and I continued living with our grandmother after Daddy Nelson died. We wanted to stay with her. We were afraid they might take us away from her and put us in an orphanage. We were very fortunate we got to stay with her. She took care of us and we tried to take care of her. We had a fabulous, blessed childhood with her. She gave us all of her: her life, her time, her knowledge of the world, her spirituality, and her devoted love.

MY NEXT-DOOR NEIGHBOR WAS MRS. BRESSLER, A DEVOUT CHRIStian lady who was very good friends with my grandmother. They lived next door to each other in Abbott all the time I was growing up there. She told me when I was about six years old that anyone who drank beer or smoked cigarettes—anyone who used alcohol or tobacco, really—was "going to hell." She really believed that, and for a while I did too. I had started drinking and smoking by the time I was six years old, so if that was true, I've been hell-bound since I was barely out of kindergarten! I would take a dozen eggs from our chicken, walk to the grocery store, and trade the dozen eggs for a pack of Camel cigarettes. I liked the little camel on the package—after all, I was only six. They were marketing directly to me! After that I liked Lucky Strikes, Chesterfields, even tried the menthol cigarettes, because they said it was a lot easier on your throat. That's a lot of horseshit. Cigarettes killed my mother, my father, my stepmother, and my stepfather—half the people in my family were killed by cigarettes. I watched my dad die after lying in bed with oxygen the last couple of years of his life. Cigarettes have killed more people than all the wars put together I think. But like my old buddy Billy Cooper used to say, "It's my mouth. I'll haul coal in it if I want to." I think I'd have been better off with the coal.

I TRIED A HUNDRED TIMES TO QUIT SMOKING. BY THE TIME I ACTU-ally did quit smoking cigarettes, I had already started smoking pot, which I picked up from a couple of old musician buddies that I had run into in Fort Worth. The first time I smoked pot I kept wait-ing for something to happen. I kept puffing and puffing, waiting for something to happen, but nothing happened. So I went back to cigarettes and whiskey, which made shit happen. As I started play-ing the clubs around Texas, I ran into the pills: the white crosses, the yellow turnarounds, and the black mollies. I never liked any of the pills or speed, because I didn't need speed; I was already speed-ing. So I quit everything but pot. Cigarettes were the hardest. My lungs were killing me from smoking everything from cedar post to grapevine, but I wasn't getting high off the cigarettes, so it was good-bye, Chesterfields, and I haven't smoked since. It's one of the best decisions I have ever made.

The day I quit, the day that I decided that I was through with fucking cigarettes, I took out the pack of cigarettes that I had just bought, opened it, threw them all away, rolled up twenty joints, replaced the twenty Chesterfields, and put the pack back in my shirt pocket, where I always kept my cigarettes, because half of the habit, for me, was reaching for and lighting something.

FAMILY BIBLE

There's a family Bible on the table
Its pages worn and hard to read
But the family Bible
On the table will ever be
My key to memories
I can see us sitting round the table
When from the family Bible Dad would read
And I can hear my mother softly singing
Rock of ages
Rock of Ages cleft for me
This old world of ours is filled with trouble
But this old world would oh so better be
If we found more Bibles on the table
And mothers singing rock of ages cleft for me

THE NIGHT OWL AND BUD FLETCHER

The Night Owl was hell—at least that's what Mrs. Bressler told me. It was the first place that my best friend, Zeke Varnon, and I used to hang out, get drunk, and play music. There was a lot of drinking, smoking, dancing, cussing, and fighting. Margie and Lundy ran the Night Owl. In the middle of all this confusion and fighting was music. It's what brought everyone there. It was one of the first beer joints that I played. Me, Sister Bobbie, Whistle Watson, and a little harelipped drummer. Bud Fletcher, who was Sister Bobbie's husband—she married him while she was a senior in high school—was a very good friend of mine. He was my first promoter/booker. He was about half hustler. We had a band called "Bud Fletcher and the Texans." We played the Night Owl, Chief Edwards, the Bloody Bucket, and every beer joint in Texas at least once. Bud was the bandleader, but he was not a musician, even though he looked like he was. He was in the band with us and he played upright bass. Well, not really *played* it. He spun it and kicked it a lot, but I never heard one note of music come out of it.

I would always hock my guitar during the week at a pawnshop in Waco and drink and gamble up all the money, and Bud would always have to go get my guitar out of hock before the weekend so we could go play our music gigs. I used to say I hocked my guitar so many times that the pawnbroker played it better than I did. But Bud would always get it out of hock, because he would have already booked us in a place, and we needed to go play.

I remember one night we played some bar for the door (meaning we got the money people paid to get in—the bar got the money from the booze). There were six of us and we each made thirty-seven cents. That was not an unusual night. We were always getting booked into places that weren't quite ready for us. I'm not saying we were bad, but our music just didn't quite fit in in places like the Scenic Wonderland in Waco, which was a huge dance hall that held about two thousand people. We could never manage to get more than twelve or fourteen people in there.

We also played a radio show each Saturday in Hillsboro at KHBR studios. It was a lot of fun, a great experience, and allowed us to plug the shows that we were playing around the state. We played in places like Whitney, West, Waco, and San Antonio.

One time, we played the Huntsville Rodeo at the Huntsville state penitentiary. As soon as we got to the property line, the guard from the penitentiary got on the bus to escort us to the bandstand. We had about twenty pounds of pot in the bay of the bus that we had bought the day before. The guard *must* have smelled it, because I did, but if he did, he never said a word. We played the rodeo, which was the best rodeo I had ever seen in my life, because these guys just didn't give a shit, and got out of there as quick as we could!

Thought for the Day: If it ain't broke, break it!

BACK TO ABBOTT

I was trimming trees with Zeke, Billy Bressier, and Curly Ingram. Curly was the boss of the tree-trimming gang. We worked for Asplundh Tree Company, which was a contractor hired by the Texas Power and Light Company to keep the power lines clear and free of trees and limbs. My job was feeding the chipper, a machine that ground up the limbs when they were thrown down from the trees, and at the end of the day, we would take the load of chips to the dump. One day, Billy Bressier was high up in a tree sawing off a limb. He needed a rope to tie around the limb so that it could be lowered to the ground without falling on anybody or anything. I climbed up the tree to give him the rope, which I had done a few times before, and instead of climbing back down the tree, I decided to climb back down the rope. I had just started down the rope when my left hand

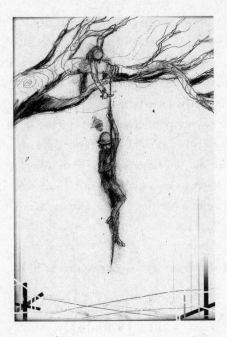

got tangled up with the rope. My fingers on my left hand were intertwined with the rope above my head where I had tried to lower myself. I was hung up. I couldn't go up, and I couldn't go down. We were about twenty feet above the ground. Right below me were the two power lines. The rope was tearing the fingers off my left hand when I told Billy to cut it. He did and I fell all the way to the ground, right between the two power lines. I hit the ground, jumped up, and walked away from that job, never to return.

> Had all my medication and it's half past ten
> I'm just sitting round waiting for something to kick in
> —WILLIE NELSON, SONG IN PROGRESS

CHURCH

I have spent all my life in church. The Bible says our body is our church, our temple, and I have spent seventy-nine years in this temple. We all live in our church.

Church is not a building; it's our body, our temple, and we should take care of our church. It's the only one we get this life-time, and we will be judged by the way we treat it. The better we treat our body, the longer, healthier the life we will have, and the more we will be able to do for the world and ourselves. We are our brother's keeper, and he is ours. Treat him the way you want to be treated. You get back what you give. Good for good, bad for bad; for every action there is an equal and opposite reaction. If you dish it out, you better be ready to take it.

Amen.

Abbott had four churches and one tabernacle, where all the other churches used to hold their summer revivals. We lived right next door, and I mean *right* next door. I could sit at our dining room table and hear every word. Baptist, Methodist, Church of Christ—great singing and preaching, and when it was the Methodists' revival, I went every night. And every time the preacher gave the invocation, where he tried to get you to admit your sins and join the church, I went down and asked for forgiveness. For what, I didn't know; I was only ten years old. How much sinning was I into at ten? But I went down anyway because it made all the women in the church happy. They loved me. They made me a lifetime member of the women's missionary society. That's a true story. The Catholic Church was a little more lenient. They danced and drank beer, and it was okay.

I played dances for the Catholics at the SPJST Hall, where they would get together, dance, play dominoes, and have fun. My first paying gig was at the SPJST Hall in West Texas, with the John Rejcek family band. They played polkas, waltzes, "Cotton-Eyed Joes," the schottische, the Bunny Hop, and the Texas two-step. I learned to play them all, and got paid for it. I made ten dollars. I had hit the big time!

SISTER BOBBIE

Our first music performances together were in our church, the Abbott Methodist Church, where we were all members. Our grandfather wasn't a regular churchgoer, but our grandmother was. She had us scrubbed and cleaned and dressed for church every time the doors opened. She was a Sunday school teacher for children as well as a music teacher for anyone who wanted to learn to read music, play an instrument, or sing. This was one of the ways we survived. She used the barter system, exchanging her knowledge of music and life for some of the material things we needed for a comfortable survival. We were never unhappy or sad because she made sure of that.

I KNOW MY PART

I know my part
I'll bring up the rear
I'll eat the dust
You know I don't care
That's what I do
I'll get 'em thru
I'm driving the herd
I sing 'em to sleep
I sing 'em awake
They like my songs
I give and I take
I know my part
I play from the heart
While I'm driving the herd
Or maybe I'm following
They let me know
If I'm doing it right
They sing along with me every night

TROUBLEMAKER

I've been called a troublemaker a time or two. What the hell is a troublemaker? you ask. Well, it's someone who makes trouble; that's what he came here to do, and that's what he does, by God. Like it or not, love it or not, he will stir it up. Why? Because it needs stirring up! If someone doesn't do it, it won't get done, and you know you love to stir it up . . . I know I do.

THE TROUBLEMAKER
—BRUCE G. BELLAND, DAVID TROY SOMERVILLE

I could tell the moment that I saw him
He was nothing but the troublemaking kind
His hair was much too long
And his motley group of friends
Had nothing but rebellion on their minds

He's rejected the establishment completely
And I know for sure he's never held a job
He just goes from town to town
Stirring up the young folks
Till they're nothing but a disrespectful mob

And I know for sure he's never joined the army
And served his country like we all have done
He'd rather wear his sandals and his flowers
While others wage a war that must be won

They arrested him last week and found him guilty
And sentenced him to die but that's no great loss
Friday they will take him to a place called Calvary
And hang that troublemaker to a cross

SALESMANSHIP

I did a lot of work in sales. I have worked selling on the radio and door-to-door—encyclopedias, vacuum cleaners, books, sewing machines, and all kinds of sales. I had my own sales crew in Waco selling the *Encyclopedia Americana*. They were and are still, I think, a great set of books. Every home should have a set, and I tried hard to put one in every home. I had great teachers, and I got good at selling them. We had a friend who worked with the phone company and who gave us all the new listings in Fort Worth each week. We called them and would make an appointment to come by their home and show them the new *Encyclopedia Americana*. We would make at least six appointments per day, then go out that night and try to make a sale. A good salesman would sell at least three sets of books out of the six appointments. The books sold for three hundred to six hundred dollars, depending on the binding. You could make from sixty to a couple hundred dollars' commission per sale. Three per night added up pretty good. But this job and all the others were just temporary until I found a job playing music.

As I said, I worked at KHBR in Hillsboro, where I had a live show with my band on Saturday at noon. It paid nothing and only covered a few miles, but my band and I could plug our dates. I also worked at KBOP in Pleasanton, KCNC in Fort Worth, and KVAN in Vancouver, Washington. It was a good way to stay involved in music.

ONE IN A ROW

If you can truthfully say that you've been true just one day
Well that makes one in a row one in a row one in a row
And if you can look into my eyes one time without telling lies
Well that makes one in a row one in a row one in a row

Why oh why do I keep loving you
After all of the things you do
And just one time come into my arms
And be glad that you're in my arms
That will make one in a row one in a row one in a row

Why oh why do I keep loving you
After all of the things you do
And just one time come into my arms
And be glad that you're in my arms
That will make one in a row one in a row one in a row

One in a row, one in a row
One in a row, one in a row

Thought for the Day: Remember, we're not happy till you're not happy.

OCCUPY WALL STREET

They are still at it, and it's been weeks. It's growing; it's good. Where and when will it end? Not until the 1 percent antes up the equivalent of what the working-class people are sacrificing. They say it's the 99 percent against the 1 percent, but I believe it is more like 99.9 percent against one-tenth of 1 percent, which equals about 1,200 people who own the world. And then there are all the rest of us who pay them to rob us blind. The one-tenth of 1 percent love to complain about welfare moms who take what amounts to chump change in funding compared to the trillions that the one-tenth of 1 percent take from our tax dollars as subsidies . . . which is nothing more than welfare. And just because you're a millionaire, or some would say *rich,* does not mean you are a crook . . . no more than you can say that everyone who is poor is completely honest. There are a lot of poor people who would like to be millionaires, regardless of what they would have to do to get there, and a lot of millionaires who have used their money for good. Some would say I am in that category, and even I believe, like Warren Buffett, that it just ain't fair for people like us to have all the advantages.

I started the TeaPot Party after I got busted for pot in Sierra Blanca, Texas. I thought, *Hey, there's a Tea Party, so why not a TeaPot Party?* There are now TeaPot Party representatives in every state of the union, and even in several foreign countries. On a few occasions, the TeaPot Party has backed a few politicians who believe, as we do, that marijuana should be legalized, taxed, and regulated the same way we do alcohol and tobacco. On the border of Mexico and the United States, thousands of people are killed annually because of the war for and against drugs. We should bring home all of our troops from around the world, put them on our borders, and legalize drugs, and in doing so we will save thousands of lives and millions of dollars. We should not be sending people to prison for smoking a joint, who after years in prison return to society as hardened criminals, with no other way to make a living than, you guessed it, selling drugs. Addiction should be treated as a disease, period.

If we legalized drugs in this country, and treated abuse as the disease it is, and offered medical treatment for these addicts, it would make much more sense than putting them in prison, and we should leave the marijuana users alone but tax them. It's already been proven that taxing and regulating marijuana makes more sense than sending young people to prison for smoking a God-given herb that has never proven to be fatal to anybody. Cigarettes and alcohol have killed millions, and there's no law against them, because again, there's a lot of money in cigarettes and alcohol. If they could realize there is just as much profit in marijuana, and they taxed and regulated it as they do cigarettes and alcohol, they could realize the same amount of profit and reduce trillions of dollars in debt. Making marijuana illegal only helps the criminals and the private prisons. My mother and my dad, my stepmother, my stepdad—well, half of my family—have been killed by cigarettes, and as far as I know, no one has ever died from smoking marijuana. Marijuana's being illegal makes no sense at all because that's not keeping it off the market. I've never had trouble getting marijuana anywhere in the world. In the places where it's legal, the smart countries, they are making a profit. And where it's *not* legal, the only people making money are the criminals.

Put something in the pot, boy; it's your move. Your back is against the wall, and that wall is Wall Street against Main Street. I didn't come here and I ain't leaving.

Amen.

LEAVING ABBOTT

We moved to Pleasanton, Texas, where I lied my way into the job at KBOP. The owner of the station was a guy named Dr. Ben Parker. Dr. Parker was a wealthy chiropractor who owned at least six radio stations in Texas. My job was to sign on in the mornings, which meant I did news and weather, played music, swept the floor, wrote copy, sold time, and collected. I did everything there was to do in a radio station, except that I was not an engineer and couldn't work on the equipment. When I applied for the job, Dr. Parker asked me if I had any experience. Of course I lied and said I did. So he asked me to sit down, go on the air, and read a commercial I had never seen. Live. I'll never forget that commercial. It was for the Pleasanton Pharmacy, and at the end of the commercial I was to say, "This program is brought to you by the Pleasanton Pharmacy, whose pharmaceutical department will accurately and precisely fill your doctor's prescription." Of course I screwed that up completely. He asked me if I was familiar with the board, which was an RCA board, because as a disc jockey I would have to operate all the equipment, turntables, and tape machines. And when Doc Parker asked me if I was familiar with this particular board, I said, "No, I was trained on a Gates board," which I had no idea about either, but I had seen it somewhere. Doc Parker must have just liked me and knew I had a family and needed a job, because he gave me the job and showed me how to operate the equipment.

I had a lot of fun at KBOP. I learned a lot about radio and how it all operates. I worked on Sunday mornings, when all the churches came in to do their Sunday morning church services at KBOP. The Church of Christ, the Baptist Church, the Methodist Church, the Catholic Church, and the Pentecostal Church, or the holy rollers as we called them, because they became so emotional and involved. They would shout, dance, and make all kinds of noise. We had to tie the chairs together because otherwise they would be thrown all over the studio. I would sit at the controls, and I could see through to the live studio where all this was going on every Sunday morning. I would always be a little hung over from Saturday night, and they obviously knew this because they all looked right directly at me and preached every word to me, it seemed like.

I did a live radio show, just me and my guitar, from noon until twelve thirty daily. This is where I first met Johnny Bush. I liked his singing well enough that I thought he needed a manager. So I became his manager, and somewhere there are still posters that say JOHNNY BUSH, MANAGED BY WILLIE NELSON. I don't think it hurt him much, because he still sings so beautiful.

Johnny was not only a good singer, but he was a good musician. He played bass and was a fine drummer. He eventually wound up playing drums for me in a three-piece band that included me, Johnny Bush, and Wade Ray. We were pretty good. We played the Panther Hall ballroom in Fort Worth, which was an old professional bowling alley that had been converted into a beer joint. The three of us recorded my first live album at the Panther Hall ballroom.

I remember one night we debuted a Beatles song called "Yesterday." The crowd loved it. I thought that I had discovered an obscure song that no one had heard of before, not realizing that the Beatles had just sold ninety zillion records.

I also thought I had discovered Julio Iglesias. I was in England on tour, listening to the BBC radio late night, and they played a song—I couldn't remember the song, but I remembered the voice and decided I had to record with this voice, whoever it was that I thought I had discovered. I found out later that he too had already sold ninety zillion records—but in seven different languages. I eventually got word to him, and we recorded "To All the Girls I've Loved Before" at my studio in Austin. It's the same studio where I recorded "Seven Spanish Angels" with Ray Charles, who is another hero of mine.

Ray Charles

Ray Charles did more for country music than anyone else. When he recorded the album *Modern Sounds in Country and Western Music,* with all the great country classics, millions of Ray Charles fans were introduced to country music. I had been a Ray Charles fan all the way back to "What'd I Say." To be able to record and sing with him was a dream come true. We eventually became good friends, and I sang many shows with him. The best one was in New York on my sixtieth birthday. Ray Charles flew in from Spain to New York, just to come sing at my birthday show, and when he and Leon Russell sang "A Song for You," it was the best I had ever heard. So thank you, Ray, and thank you, Leon.

The greatest musician, singer, writer, and entertainer that I have ever seen or heard is Leon Russell. We are still great friends and have a double album of songs that we recorded, called *Together Again,* coming out next year. I first saw Leon in Albuquerque, New Mexico. There were twenty thousand people on their feet yelling and screaming for the whole show. He and I stayed up all night the night before the show drinking and smoking. At sunrise we went onstage and started playing. It was the greatest sight I had ever seen. There were thousands of people walking toward the venue through a cow pasture, carrying everything from beer coolers to sleeping bags. They came to stay a while. There were hippies and rednecks, young and old coming together for the first time to hear the same thing. The magic was the music. It touched all kinds of people, and the world has not been the same since. I remember he had the crowd in such a frenzy that at one moment he stopped and said, "Remember where you are right now, and remember that right now you would believe anything I would say. So be careful who you would let lead you to this place." Then he threw his cowboy hat into the audience, and the crowd went crazy, which is when I stole the idea of throwing hats to the audience.

I booked Leon for the first Fourth of July picnic in Dripping Springs, Texas. I thought if it worked in Albuquerque and it worked in Woodstock, it could work here; it did. Thank you, Leon, and thank you, Woodstock, for showing me how to do it.

Leon Russell

ALWAYS NOW

It's always now
Nothing ever goes away
Everything is here to stay
And it's always now
It's always now
There never was a used to be
Everything is still with me
And it's always now
So brace your heart
And save yourself some sanity
It's more than just a memory
And it's always now
And here's your part
Sing it like a melody

There's really only you and me
And it's always now

NASHVILLE

I went to Nashville because Nashville was *the* marketplace, and if you wanted to succeed in country music you had to go to Nashville—so I went to Nashville. I drove there from Houston in a '51 Buick. I had been teaching guitar at Paul Buskirk's music studio. I taught a class where I had about twelve full-time students. I loved teaching guitar. I could play pretty good, so I would knock out a few blues licks to impress the class, then jump into Mel Bay's book and teach little fingers to play. It was and still is a great way to teach. By the time you went through the first book, you had learned a lot about reading music, and I was learning as much as I was teaching.

I had just recorded "Night Life" with Paul Buskirk's band. He was the best rhythm guitar player I had ever heard. Dean "Deanie Bird" Reynolds played great upright bass, and I played lead guitar. I had also just written "Family Bible," which was recorded by Claude Gray. I sold the song for fifty dollars, because I needed the money to pay my rent. The song went to No. 1 on the *Billboard* charts. So when I hit Nashville, I had a record and a No. 1 song.

I met Hank Cochran at a bar called Tootsie's Orchid Lounge, which is right across the alley from the Ryman Auditorium, the home of the Grand Ole Opry. All the artists and musicians who played the Grand Ole Opry would spend a lot of time at Tootsie's. It's where I met Faron Young, who turned out to be a great friend and who recorded my song "Hello Walls," which became his biggest hit.

Tootsie's was also where I met Charlie Dick, who was married to the great Patsy Cline. He heard and liked one of my records on the jukebox, so I played him a tape of "Crazy." He took me to Patsy's house and woke her up so she could hear it, too. I remember I was embarrassed to go into their house—it was past midnight—so I stayed in the car. She came out and made me come in, and she recorded "Crazy" the next week. It was the biggest jukebox song of all time.

Back to Hank Cochran—Hank heard me jamming with Jimmy Day and Buddy Emmons one night in Tootsie's. He was a writer for Pamper Music, which was owned by Ray Price and Hal Smith. Also, there were Harlan Howard, Ray Pennington, Don Rollins, and Dave Kirby. All great writers. Hank had a fifty-dollar-a-week raise coming but told Hal Smith to hire me as a writer and give me the fifty dollars-a-week instead. It was fantastic, and I thought I had hit the big time!

There is a new singer in town who has a great voice and a good heart and is doing really well. His name is Jamey Johnson, and he is doing an album of Hank Cochran songs. Hank wrote some great songs, like "Make the World Go Away" and "A Little Bitty Tear." We did one the other night that I had only recently heard for the first time called "Livin' for a Song." It was me, Jamey, and Kris Kristofferson singing on that one. I'm glad Jamey is kicking the can on down the road, so people don't forget Hank and people like him. Thank you, Hank, wherever you are.

Thought for the Day: You have all the power there is. There is no one more powerful than you. You just must be aware of it and know it; don't doubt it. Faith, dummy. (Those last two words were for me.)

THINK IT. BE IT. YOU ARE THE SUM TOTAL OF ALL YOUR THOUGHTS. Remember you are who you wanted to be. If you're happy, thank God and move on. If you want to change, you can. Intentions are important, but remember you can kill yourself with good intentions. If everything fails, start over. Failure is not fatal. It's inevitable that you learn from your mistakes. If you fail, you start over. If you fail again, you start over again. If you fall seven times, get up eight. Amen. Or om, or . . . ?

I can still see the Abbott Panther motto: "A quitter never wins, and a winner never quits." Abbott High School was the greatest school in the world for me and small enough that I could take every subject. You will pass some and fail some, but the ones you fail you will remember longer. Kind of like in life, you keep coming back till you get it right, or as someone said, "Keep doing it wrong till you like it that way." I think I already said that, but it's important.

BASS 101

The best country singer of all time was, and still is, Ray Price. His bass player Donny Young, who later became Johnny Paycheck, quit and I was hired to replace him. I had never played bass in my life, but when Ray asked me if I could play bass I said, "Can't everybody?" Jimmy Day tried to teach me on the way from Nashville to Winchester, Virginia, which was Patsy Cline's hometown. It was a struggle for us both. Johnny Bush played drums for Ray, but I played bass, so he was screwed from the get-go. I asked Ray later how long it took him to realize I was no bass player. He said the first night, but he kept me around, so thank you, Ray.

Ray had his band dressed in pink and blue Nudie suits with sequins. Donny was about fifty pounds lighter than I was, so the suit was a little snug, but after a while on the bus eating truck-stop food, it began to fit better. I opened with the band and sang a few Hank Williams songs and told a couple of Little Jimmy Dickens's jokes. Then I would introduce Ray. Most of the way through my show there was a lot of heckling, like "Where's Ray? We paid to see Ray Price!" It was a very humbling experience. I understood very well what they meant, and I too was glad when Ray came on. Later, when Johnny Bush opened for me, he had to listen to, "Where's Willie? We paid to see Willie!" It's all funny now. We actually have a new CD called *Young at Heart* coming out next year. Here I go plugging my music again. Bite me.

Ray Price helped us out on the CD and sang great, as usual, but he's been a little under the weather lately. He told me he had to cut back. His exact words were "I'm only living six days a week now." Now *that's* funny!

RAISING HOGS

I spent some great years living in Tennessee. I first lived in Dunn's Trailer Park in Madisonville, Tennessee, just north of Nashville. Roger Miller and Hank Cochran both lived there at one time for no reason that I can think of, except that it was twenty-five dollars a week, with everything furnished. Not such a bad deal.

Then I bought a farm in Ridgetop, Tennessee, which was some of the best and worst of times.

When I was married to Shirley Collie, we lived in Ridgetop, and Johnny Bush lived close by. One day, I decided to quit touring—I literally took myself off the market, because the only place I was doing good at all was in Texas—and to stay home a year to write songs and raise hogs. Why hogs? Because I had been raising hogs nearly all my life, starting out in the FFA at Abbott High School, where I raised hogs for show, food, money, or whatever. I even won some blue ribbons. So it wasn't unusual for me to decide

I wanted to raise hogs in my year off with nothing to do. I got Johnny Bush to help me build a hog pen. Then we went to the auction sale over in Goodlettsville, where I bought seventeen weaner pigs. I paid twenty-five cents a pound, put them in the back of my pickup, drove back to Ridgetop with Johnny, backed the pickup truck up to the loading gate, and unloaded the pigs in the pigpen we had just built. Unfortunately, the bottom rung on the pigpen was about two inches higher than the tallest hog. Consequently, all seventeen pigs hit the ground running. They went straight out under the fence and separated out in the woods. It took us days to finally round up all the pigs. By the time we got them back in the pen, they were almost too big to crawl out again, but we fixed the bottom of the pen and I started raising hogs. Another mistake I had made was having the hog feeders and the water trough too close together in the hog pen. The pigs wouldn't get any exercise because they didn't have to walk and got so fat, they were rupturing—they were literally falling out of their own asses. Long story short, I fed the seventeen pigs for three months and took them to the market to sell them, and the hogs that I had paid twenty-five cents a pound for—and had fed for ninety days—brought only twenty cents a pound. I lost a minor fortune my first and only year raising hogs.

ROPING

During that same year I decided I would build a roping arena, and with the help of Johnny Bush, again, I did.

Johnny is a good friend. He played drums for me one time, fronted my band, and now he was helping me put up an electric fence. *That's* a real friend. But to show you how bright we were,

Johnny and I dug the holes, drove in the metal fence posts, and put up the wiring for an electric fence during a thunder and lightning storm. I was riding my black quarter horse Preacher, whom I dearly loved, over toward the roping pen we had just built, and when we got to the electric fence, Johnny Bush lowered the wire. My idea was to ride Preacher over the electric fence while Johnny Bush held the wire down to the ground. When we were halfway across the wire, John let it go, accidentally I'm sure. Hence the first Ridgetop Rodeo!

I had never roped calves before, but I knew it had to be a lot of fun. I bought a book called *Calf Roping* by Toots Mansfield. Toots was a many-times-over champion roper from West Texas. He had a calf-roping school that he ran in either Midland or Big Spring, Texas. He had a lot of young calf ropers to whom he taught the finer skills of roping, so I was sure I could learn from his book. I studied it and read it over many times until I was sure I knew what I had to do. I was to catch a running calf by throwing a loop over his head, throwing the calf, dismounting the horse, and tying the calf's feet together, in as short a time period as possible. Unfortunately, my roping horse Preacher had not read the book.

DID YOU HEAR ABOUT THE NERVOUS BANK ROBBER? HE SAID: "STICK up your ass or I'll blow your hands off!"

IT WAS CHRISTMASTIME, AND THE LADY ANSWERED THE DOOR. IT was the postman. She said, "Come in, I have something for you." She took him to the bedroom and screwed his brains out, then fixed him a nice big breakfast of biscuits, gravy, ham, and eggs. Then she walked him to the door, gave him a dollar, and said, "Merry Christmas." The postman said, "Lady, what just happened?" She said, "I asked my husband what to give you for Christmas, and he said, 'Fuck him, give him a dollar.' Breakfast was my idea."

I DID AN INTERVIEW TODAY WITH AN OLD FRIEND FROM SAN ANTO-nio named Paul Venema. He's a great guy and an old friend. I'll see him tomorrow night in Helotes, Texas, at our show at John T. Floore Country Store. John T's is one of the better beer joints in Texas. John T. Floore was a really good friend of mine and loaned me money one time when I really needed it. I wrote a song about him:

SHOTGUN WILLIE

Shotgun Willie sits around in his underwear
Biting on a bullet and pulling out all of his hair
Shotgun Willie's got all of his family there

Well, you can't make a record if you ain't got nothing to say
You can't make a record if you ain't got nothing to say
You can't play music if you don't know nothing to play

Shotgun Willie sits around in his underwear
Biting on a bullet and pulling out all of his hair
Shotgun Willie's got all of his family there

Now, John T. Floore was a-working for the Ku Klux Klan
At six foot five, John T. was a hell of a man
Made a lot of money selling sheets on the family plan

Shotgun Willie sits around in his underwear
Biting on a bullet and pulling out all of his hair
Shotgun Willie's got all of his family there

MAUI, SUMMER 2011

Annie and I are on Maui having fun. The weather is perfect; it usually is. Texas was getting a little warm, but Maui feels fantastic. Jim Fuller and I played chess and dominoes today. We will play golf in the morning. Jim is one of my best friends. He used to own a restaurant called Charley's in the town of Paia, on the North Shore of Maui. I played music there a lot and had a lot of fun. Jim is not only a good friend but a good poker player, and a pretty good golfer now. I know he took some lessons, because I used to give him two strokes a hole and now he beats me a lot. One day I was playing golf and won Charley's! Of course I immediately lost it back. I don't need a restaurant.

Jim and I play chess and dominoes together. I hope to see him tomorrow night in Django's, my clubhouse, or man cave, where we play all sorts of games, like poker, dominoes, and chess. Stan Cohn, Ben Holtz, Big Ben, Donny Smith, Roy, and Joe Gannon are regulars. Ziggy Marley showed up for a game and won a bunch. Then his wife, Orly, said they had to leave to take the kids home. Right . . . we will get Ziggy back! Anyway, all my pals will be there. I will win some and lose some, but at least I don't have to fly to Vegas!

Jim Sanders is another really good friend of mine, and one

of our regular poker players. Jim has been around the world nine times and remembers everything. He is a great storyteller and wonderful human.

Don Nelson, or "Nellie" as we call him, will be at the poker game as well. We are both Hall of Famers—he in the NBA, me in the Country Music—but we still remain humble. We are not conceited—although we have every right to be!

THE HEIGHT OF CONCEIT IS A FLEA FLOATING DOWN THE RIVER ON HIS back with a hard-on, yelling, "Raise the drawbridge!"

Donny Smith will play poker with us tomorrow night. He is a good friend and a great guitar player; we have played shows together several times.

Sometimes Woody Harrelson and Owen Wilson play poker with us, but they are off the island somewhere for now. Woody has a new play that just opened off-Broadway called Bullet for Adolf—*I hear it is doing really well—and Owen is off making a movie somewhere, but I wish they could be here. They could at least send money.*

I HAD A LITTLE CONSTIPATION PROBLEM THE OTHER DAY, SO THE doctor gave me some of them suppositories. For all the good they done I might as well have stuck 'em up my ass!

A GUY AND HIS WIFE HAD BEEN MARRIED FIFTY YEARS AND HAD played golf together every day for those fifty years. This day was their fiftieth wedding anniversary. They were on the tee box, and the wife said, "Honey, why don't we confess all our sins right here and start the next fifty years with a clean slate?" The husband said, "Okay, honey. Do you remember that pretty blond secretary I had about seventeen years ago? Well, I had an affair with her." The wife said, "Oh, that's okay, honey, the year before I met you I had a sex change." The husband said, "Why, you lying whore! All this time you've been hitting from the red tees!"

Oh well, you win some, you lose some, and some get rained out; that's an Abbottism for you literary types.

IF A FROG HAD WINGS HE COULD GET BIRD PUSSY. IF YOUR SISTER HAD balls, she would be your brother.

It's getting late. It's two twenty-five A.M. Maui time. Signing off, aloha and mahalo.

I am in Hawaii again today with my family, counting my blessings . . . oh yeah, that and the money I won last night playing poker.

Django's Orchid Lounge is my little hideout on the ocean, with poker, chess, and domino tables. Our sign says, LIQUOR UP FRONT—POKER IN THE REAR and HIPPIES USE THE SIDE DOOR! My brother-in-law Joe D'Angelo named it Django's Orchid Lounge since he knows how much I love Django Reinhardt—and it actu-

ally used to be an orchid house. He had the sign made up as a gift to me, and the name stuck. For those who don't know, Django Reinhardt is the greatest guitar player who ever lived. He was born in a Gypsy wagon in Belgium. When he was a young boy, the wagon caught fire. His left hand was burned so bad he only had two fingers and a thumb to play with. But he did more with two fingers and a thumb than any other guitar player has ever done. He's my guitar hero, so that's why the lounge was named after him, just to keep his name alive. Every July there is a Django Reinhardt Festival in the South of France, which I will get to someday!

From where I am now on Maui, I can see six palm trees dancing on the water like six slender ladies. Plus an old monkey pod tree. That one monkey pod tree reminds me of the trees I grew up with in Abbott: the scrub oaks and cedar, the cottonwood tree in my yard that I loved to climb, and the tree in Aquilla Creek that we used to tie a rope to so we could swing out and drop into the water on Sunday afternoon . . . after the bumblebee fights. Our house in Abbott—the one we moved to after we lived at the house with the cottonwood tree—has seventeen pecan trees growing all around it. I don't know if they still produce pecans, but they used to a few storms ago. And that's all I'm going to say about trees.

AUSTIN, TEXAS, AUGUST 2011

We finally got some rain on the day I was going to finally get to ride my horse. One-hundred-degree weather for over seventy days is a little hard on the horse—and this old cowboy too. We were going to make a video for the song "A Horse Called Music."

37

I was going to ride through town on my horse Billy Boy, but no, it rained. Oh well, maybe tomorrow.

If at first you don't succeed . . . fuck it!

SEPTEMBER 2011

I'm riding my horse Billy Boy around the town of Luck, in the heart of the great state of Texas. Why do Texans brag? They are just telling the truth.

We got to make our "A Horse Called Music" video, and I had a lot of fun doing it. The world looks better on a horse.

NOVEMBER 16, 2011

Annie just got home. She and Sister Bobbie went to see Aretha Franklin tonight at Austin City Limits Live at the Moody Theater. They said she was still so great. Her recording of

"Night Life" is so good, and I'm sorry I didn't get to see her with them . . . oh well.

Annie and I have oral sex all the time. When we pass each other in the hallway I say, "Fuck you," and she says, "Fuck you more." Love like that never dies!

OCCUPY WALL STREET UPDATE #2

"Anyone who can remain calm in all this confusion just doesn't understand the situation."

I love Howard Zinn. Here's one of my favorite quotes of his:

> Civil disobedience is not our problem. Our problem is civil obedience. Our problem is that people all over the world have obeyed the dictates of leaders . . . and millions have been killed because of this obedience. . . . Our problem is that people are obedient all over the world in the face of poverty and starvation and stupidity, and war, and cruelty. Our problem is that people are obedient while the jails are full of petty thieves . . . [and] the grand thieves are running the country. That's our problem.
>
> —HOWARD ZINN

There's really only you and me, and it's always now.

—WILLIE NELSON

GOD HATES FAGS

God hates fags
That's what the sign said
God hates signs . . . God said
It's a sign of the times
I said.

IN GOD'S EYES

Never think evil thoughts of anyone
It's just as wrong to think as to say
For a thought is but a word that's unspoken
In God's eyes He sees it this way

Lend a hand if you can to a stranger
Never worry if he can't repay
For in time you'll be repaid ten times over
In God's eyes He sees it this way

In God's eyes we're like sheep in a meadow
Now and then a lamb goes astray
But open arms should await its returning
In God's eyes He sees it this way

Thought for the Day: Sometimes I think, Well . . . then again I don't know, but when you get right down to it, there it is.

NOW BACK TO THE FARMERS

I see where three hundred thousand farmers are suing Monsanto, and someone said I was involved in the lawsuit, which I'm not, but I totally approve of it. And if it gets to the court they can call me and I will tell them exactly what I think about these industrial ag corporations who are poisoning the earth and putting farmers off the land, not only in America but also around the world.

BioWillie Biodiesel

Quality fuel made in America

BioWillie Biodiesel—a petroleum diesel alternative made from waste vegetable oil, waste fats, and seed oil crops

We have in America all the energy we need to run our country. We have hydro, solar, wind, and biodiesel, not to mention all the oil and gas still in the ground, but we are ignoring it all to go around the world starting wars to steal other people's resources. Is it about oil or is it about starting wars? I think it's both. I think there's a lot of money in war. And as my ole buddy George W. says, "Money trumps peace." It is assumed by the so-called 1 percent that there is more money in oil and war than there is in peace. That there is more money in oil and war for the people who own the oil and for defense contractors, who start and profit from all the wars. But I believe the opposite. I believe that this country would be better off bringing all of our troops home and putting them on our own borders to stop the trafficking of guns, drugs, and people. This is our major problem. All the money that's involved in this kind of trafficking and the privatization of prisons is the problem. Then again . . . money trumps common sense.

"If you don't stand for something, you'll fall for anything."

We are what we wanted to be. We are the sum total of all our thoughts. If you don't like who you are, change it. Change is just a thought away. Fake it till you make it, and one day you will be that person you wanted to be. If you like where you are, thank God and move on.

If you don't like my face, fuck it . . . oh, you know . . . moving on.

FARM AID

The Farm Aid concerts started twenty-five years ago, when a governor and a group of entertainers decided to try to help the small family farmers who were being forced off their land to make room for subdivisions and golf courses. The big corporate, industrial agricultural farmers started taking the farms away from the small family farmers. We all thought that if the powers that be in Washington knew what was going on, they would fix it. As it turned out, the deck was stacked against the small family farmer. If the corporate farmers wanted the land, they got it.

So for twenty-five years, hundreds of entertainers have paid their own way to Farm Aid to perform for free for the family farmers they wanted to help save, because they could see what was happening to our food system and wanted to stop it. The whole twenty-five years, industrial ag farms were taking more and more small family farms, and little changed.

It is plain to see now that the people in Washington are very happy with the way things are going. At one time we had had eight million small family farmers. Today there are less than two million small family farmers on the land, and we are still losing the few who are left. As I mentioned before, the deck was stacked.

Around $40 million has been raised and given to the farm groups who are trying to help farmers who have already lost their farms as well as the ones who are left to fight the battle for us all. We tried, and a lot of farmers have received much-needed help. The farmers have been very thankful for what Farm Aid has been doing, and they thank all the singers and musicians who gave their talent over the years.

God bless the small family farmer, and the millions of people in this country who have tried to help them.

There are other parts of the world where the family farms have already all been taken, and when the governments tried to give the land back after realizing they did not know how to farm, the people said, "No, you got it, now it's yours." This could happen here one day.

> *Living in the now they say*
> *But you really can't do it any other way*
> *Even if now all you do is dream of yesterday*
> *You're still living in the now*

—WILLIE NELSON

GUNS

The first gun I owned was a stick gun that went "Bang!" when I pulled the trigger. After that we made rubber guns. Rubber guns could hurt. Then I got a Daisy Red Ryder air rifle and took aim at tin cans, birds, and rabbits. Lucky for the birds and rabbits I was a bad shot, so rarely did I kill anything. When I was twelve I got a twelve-gauge shotgun. After that it was a four ten over-and-under and a deer gun—an Ithaca with a scope. I still couldn't hit anything!

I had a good shot at a bear one time in Wyoming, but thankfully I missed him twice. I eventually got a .22, then a .357 Magnum when I was only twenty. I almost shot myself twice with that fucking pistol! I sat down one time in a motel room with a bunch of people. It somehow cocked itself, so when I sat down, it fired. But the bullet missed my leg and hit the floor. Everybody thought they were shot! I have not had great experiences with guns, so I hung 'em up before I killed somebody, something, or myself.

Guitar players can drink way too much—well, at least this one did. Abbott was in Hill County, and Hill County was a dry county, but right next door in West, which was McClennan County, it was not, so you could just go buy beer at the beer joints there. West was where I picked up my first paying gigs at the Night Owl, Albert's Place, Chief Edwards's Place, and Shadowland. By the time I had graduated from high school, I had already been playing all over West and Waco, and had developed quite a following for a sixteen-year-old. My first fan club was started by a few of the girls in Hillsboro (Barbara Jean McDermen, Claudia Moore, Joyce Epps, Florabell Turner). They bought me a nice suit to wear at my graduation from Abbott High School, which they all attended as members of my fan club. As you can probably understand, it was difficult to remain humble. But I digress. Where was I? Oh yeah, guns.

All the talk now about gun control, I really understand. At the time the Second Amendment was conceived, all we had were one-shot muzzle-loading rifles. It was a different time. Now there are guns that can fire a hundred shots in less than a minute. Anyone with loved ones knows those should be outlawed. Those kinds of weapons were made only to kill people. I don't know of any serious hunter who would use this kind of firepower to hunt. It is completely unsportsmanlike. A handgun, a shotgun, and a deer rifle are all we really need. Period. End of story.

DOMINOES

I learned to play dominoes starting at the age of maybe five or six, and have played steadily ever since. There were domino parlors all over Abbott, a small town of three hundred or less. There was a table in Kiblinger's store and tables in every cotton gin office—everyone I knew in Abbott played dominoes. I learned by standing around the tables watching the old men play. Four-handed partner games were common, and when one of them would have to get up for any reason, they would let me sit in their place, so I learned pretty quick, because I knew if I played wrong I would get my ass chewed out.

There were things about dominoes you needed to know. First of all, there are twenty-eight dominoes in the deck, and there are seven suits: blank, ace, deuce, trey, four, five, and six. There are one hundred and sixty-eight spots total, which is not really important to know; I'm just showing off. What *is* important to know are the basic dos and don'ts. The dos are: take all counts and kill all doubles, except the ones in your hand. The don't would be: never play a suit that you have none of, if you can help it. We played to two hundred and fifty as the score. Now these days, over here in Hawaii, with Owen and Woody, they like to play to one hundred and fifty, which helps the less experienced domino player (insult intended). If chess is the game of kings, then dominoes is the game of hustlers and gamblers. In Abbott, when the old men were playing, it wasn't for money. It was for the pride of beating your opponent; money wasn't necessary. There was as much value in the pride of beating someone who was a good player as there was in winning any money. But mainly these old guys didn't really have any money, just their pensions, which they weren't going to throw away in a domino game. But they sure could play dominoes.

The world-championship domino tournament, which I instigated, was in West, Texas. I had all the entrants play against each other in head-up dominoes, and whoever won, I would play them for the championship . . . which guaranteed me number two domino player in the world, even if I lost. I applied the same theory to the world-championship calf-roping tournament in San Antonio. Again, I was second in the world! There were a lot of great domino players—well, there *are* a lot of great domino players—but the best domino player may have been my old buddy Zeke Varnon.

Zeke and I ran together for a long time in Texas. We worked together, drank together, gambled together, and fought together for over fifty years. One time Zeke and I were in Waco, and I left him in my car while I went into the house to pick up my girlfriend. I had just filled the car up with gas, and the guy who put the gas in had let the tank overflow onto the car. While I was in the house, Zeke was in the car asleep, or passed out, in the backseat, and some kid walked up and saw the gas leaking out of the car and yelled to Zeke in the car, "So what do you think would happen if I strike a match to this gas?" Zeke, startled, said, "Don't do that, the son of a bitch will burn up!" The kid did it anyway. Next thing I know Zeke rushes into the house screaming, "Willie, come out, the car's on fire!" My prized 1946 Ford burned to the ground, and I ended up selling it as junk for $25. I never did find that kid.

Another time with Zeke and me, this time at the Night Owl in West, there was a guy sitting at a table in the back drunk and passed out. He had fallen on the floor. Zeke went over to him, leaned down, doubled up his fists, and said, "Motherfucker, you get up and I'll hit you again!" That was Zeke.

One time, Zeke passed out and our friend Billy Bressier went through his pockets and stole two dollars. Zeke came to and saw what had happened. He grabbed a baseball bat and chased Billy all over the domino hall.

I loved Zeke!

JOKES FOR DRUNKS

A drunk went into the bar and asked another drunk what time it was.

The first drunk looked at his watch and said, "It's thirteen o'clock."

The second drunk said, "My God, let's get out of here, it's later than it's ever been!"

A drunk fell out of a second-floor window.

A guy came running over and asked, "What happened?"

The drunk said, "I don't know, I just got here."

A man came out of an antique store carrying a large grandfather clock. He bumped into a drunk and busted the grandfather clock into a thousand pieces.

The guy said, "Why don't you watch where you're going?"

The drunk said, "Why don't you wear a wristwatch like every-body else?"

A couple was making out on the second floor of a house of ill repute.

They got a little too close to the window, fell out on the side-walk, and just kept going. A drunk knocked on the door of the house of ill repute and the madam came to the door. The drunk said, "Excuse me, ma'am, but your sign fell down."

A drunk was lying on the street with his head in the gutter. A priest saw him, came over and reached down, pointed his finger in the drunk's face, and said, "You're going to h–e–l–l because you are d–r–u–n–k."

The drunk looked up at him and said, "And you are going to h–e–l–l because your finger smells like p–u–s–s–y!"

THE BANK ROBBER SAID, "STICK 'EM UP." THE CLERK SAID, "STICK what up?" The bank robber said, "Don't confuse me, this is my first job."

BEE MAN

DECEMBER 8, 2011

> Lost Bee man today
> He said the world is too crazy
> And he just passed away
> He was so tired of living that he died every day
> Lost the Bee Man today

> This was not a good day. The Bee Man died today, the world economy sucks, and it looks like a long winter. Twenty million people are out of work. It all started when we began taking the

small family farms away. We began moving farmers off the land
so we could build golf courses and subdivisions, and sold them
to people who couldn't afford them. Big corporations took over
everything, polluting the land with chemicals and fertilizers. Oh
well, what does it matter what I think? Who gives a damn really?
By the time this book comes out, me and Bee Man will probably
be back together playing music, and the world as we knew it will
be gone. Our so-called elected officials will enslave us all unless we
grow some big balls and throw all the bastards out who can't seem
to remember who it is they actually work for. You can be president and I'll help you, or I'll be president and you can help
me clean house. *That is of course if it matters one hill of beans*
who *the president is. I believe the president has no real power*
anymore. I believe Congress has no balls. Maybe they even love it
the way it is. It's kind of like Texas, where no one is in control.

In Fort Worth around Christmastime, I would see a guy
with no legs. He had roller skates on his knees, and he sold pencils,
wrapping paper, and Christmas cards. I wrote this song about him:

PRETTY PAPER

Pretty paper pretty ribbons of blue
Wrap your presents to your darling from you
Pretty pencils to write I love you
Oh pretty paper pretty ribbons of blue

There he sits all alone on the sidewalk
Hoping that you won't pass him by
Should you stop better not much too busy
You'd better hurry my how time does fly
And in the distance the ringing of laughter
And in the midst of the laughter he cries

Pretty paper pretty ribbons of blue
Wrap your presents to your darling from you
Pretty pencils to write I love you
Oh pretty paper pretty ribbons of blue

NEW YEAR'S DAY, 2012

Yesterday was quite a day. Bee's memorial service started at noon in Luck, Texas, at the church. There were a lot of great shots, clips, and stories of Bee just being Bee . . . priceless.

Bee Man was a very funny guy who would do anything for a laugh. One time in Vegas, we played a casino where Mary Poppins had been staged just before we arrived and they still had all the flying equipment. I was singing "Angel Flying Too Close to the Ground," and in the middle of my guitar solo, the people started laughing and laughing. I thought they were laughing at my guitar solo, which was, I thought, good but not funny. I looked up behind me just in time to see Bee flying across the stage. It was the funniest thing I had ever seen, and I think it still is. God bless the Bee Man.

Bee Man

FAMILY

I would like to brag on the family a little. The poster says WILLIE NELSON AND FAMILY, which really covers a lot of territory, because it consists of my sister, Bobbie; my wife, Annie; my children, Lana, Susie, Paula, Amy, Lukas, and Micah; my grandchildren, Nelson, Bryan, Rachel, Martha, Rebecca, Anthony, and Raelyn; and my great-grandchildren, Andrea, Dean, Zack, Brody, Aiden, Vivien, Ira, and Isabella.

My daughters: Lana, Paula, Susie, and Amy

The Fowler grandchildren: Rachel, Martha, Bryan, and Nelson

SUSIE NELSON

The art of the Holy Spirit is in the song. To go to my father's concerts is a loving experience. Everyone is singing along to his songs. Out in the crowd, it's a revelation. There are a lot of hugs out there. His 1960s recordings, I really enjoy. You do not hear arrangements like that anymore.

The gospel music, like "Family Bible," is the Holy Spirit of God in action. My father's been moving pretty fast. I enjoy what he does. I would have never known so many people or learned about their different personalities. There are things that I would have never known anything about, like the importance of the farmers, the seeds, our food, and our water. He really cares for his horses. One day an old truck pulled into Luck with fifty sad, skinny horses. Now they are fat and sassy with plenty of spirit!

One evening, I wanted to add water to a horse bowl, so I entered the pen. The moon was shining bright and allowed enough light to see to pour the water. The horse got spooked and ran to be by my side. With his huge body, he gently moved me out of danger. I will never forget that. I will never know what spooked him or what he was saving me from. The horses are special. I am happy to get to know them, and my father is right: "the horse is human!"

I would have never known about biodiesel fuel,

the importance of clean air, and peace on earth. Willie's grandchildren Rebecca and Anthony enjoy his ranch, and his music and movies. His great-grandson Zack is now singing. He has given me a lot to be grateful for.

Susie Nelson and Willie's grandson
Anthony Brewster

I've always thought his red bandanna was the image of the crown of thorns Jesus wore on the cross. I love the bus and how he shares it with his fans, allowing them to come on and talking with them and signing autographs. Then they are gone. It's quiet now. Everyone is watching TV like nothing ever happened that evening! As if there was not an aisle full of people all talking about the same thing . . . his music.

Willie's granddaughter Rebecca with her husband, Chris, and Willie's great-grandson Zack

It is an amazing experience, and by faith and grace are we saved. To travel as much as my father does, to sing three hours each night, to travel hundreds of miles each day, to sign autographs for a long time after his concerts, then go record for three days. It's amazing to watch. The art of the Holy Spirit is in the songs and the movies he has made. *Songwriter* was the one film where I had the revelation that he was famous. Maybe it was because it was Nashville and that he was a record executive, but that was his part. So I had to let go of wondering what he was doing next. Daughters are funny; they like to know where their fathers are from time to time.

• • •

MARY HANEY WAS MY OLD AND DEAR FRIEND FROM LONG AGO. Turns out Mary and I had a child together called Renee, who has a daughter, Noelle, who has a daughter, Jordan, who is a beautiful young girl that I am proud to call my great-granddaughter. My newly discovered family took a while to surface, and when it did, it was a surprise. Mary was a sweet lady, and I'm glad we had a family together. She would be very proud of them all. So that makes an even bigger bunch of great kids that would make any parent very proud, and they all are very smart . . . naturally.

Beyond my blood relatives are a group of friends who make up the rest of Willie Nelson and Family.

Paul English, one of my best friends for fifty years at least, is still a member of the band, along with Billy English on drums. Billy is Paul's brother who took over for Paul when he was sick. Paul is back now and playing great.

My daughter Renee with her family

PAUL ENGLISH

I first met Willie through my older brother Oliver. They had booked a job and didn't have a drummer. I played trumpet, but I had never played drums before. I told them I could do it. Later on I found out I had the beat backward! They found a Coke crate and put it on a chair for me to use as a drum stool. They gave me a snare, and then way later I got a bass drum and a sock cymbal. I just counted either a one-two-three-four beat or a one-two-three beat. I remember Paul Buskirk coming to Willie's house, and every night Paul, Willie, and myself recorded every song for Willie's radio show. Our special guest every night was Lana Nelson. She was two years old. She was a beautiful child, and she is beautiful now. After a couple of weeks we got a job at the Hemphill Club, which paid us eight dollars, three nights a week. We had another front man (I don't remember who), so Willie just played lead guitar and sang on a few songs. Willie spoke up for me when they first got the job because they were trying to figure out who to use for a drummer, and Willie said, "I think we ought to use Paul. He's been playing with us all this time for nothing."

I remember one night we were going home from the Hemphill Club and we drove up to Willie's house, which was this little side apartment. I sat and waited a minute to make sure he got in. Then I knew he got in because I heard a loud noise, which was pots and pans being thrown at him by Martha, his wife. She ran him out of the house, and about that time I figured I'd better leave. We worked for about a month at the Hemphill Club, and then the owner sold it. Me and the other band members went out to play at another club on the Jacksboro Highway. Willie went to a better job than that, but we stayed friends, and I sold him a car. I own a car lot, but I didn't have one good enough on the lot, so I went somewhere else and found one. I paid $150 for it, got the title and license, and sold it to Willie for $175, with a $25 down payment. Ten years later Willie was playing with Johnny Bush, and I was living in Houston. They would come over to my house every time they came into town.

One night Willie was asking me if I knew how to get hold of Tommy Roznoski, this other drummer, because Johnny Bush had been playing drums behind Willie, but Johnny wanted to go to the front and sing, and so he needed a drummer to fill in while he was singing. I said that I could play drums better than Roznoski anyway. Willie said, "Well, you wouldn't work for thirty dollars a day, would you?" I said, "I would," and here I am still today. I am so grateful to Willie for keeping me on and making me a part of this adventure that has been our lives. I played my first job with Willie, and I will play my last with him too.

MICKEY RAPHAEL, THE BEST HARMONICA PLAYER EVER! HE HAS BEEN playing harmonica with me since he was basically a child. He can play anything—country, rock, jazz, you name it. I ran into him in Dallas at a Coach Darrell Royal party. I asked him to come play a benefit with me, and he has been with me ever since. He is a really good picker and a really good friend.

MICKEY RAPHAEL

In 1972 I got a message from Darrell Royal, the coach of the University of Texas football team. He said he was having a little picking session in his hotel suite after the Texas-Arkansas ball game and asked me to bring my harmonicas and jam with some friends of his.

Coach was a serious music fan and patron of the arts. I was a struggling musician and had been playing in Dallas and Austin with B. W. Stevenson and Jerry Jeff Walker. The coach had seen me play and thought I'd fit in with his famous after-game jam sessions.

The coach and his wife, Edith, were very welcoming and introduced me to some of the musicians. Willie Nelson happened to be one of the guests. I didn't grow up listening to country music, although I owned one Willie Nelson record. By the end of the evening, I was a huge fan.

Willie was playing the classic songs "Night Life," "Funny How Time Slips Away," and "Crazy," and I would try to play along. His guitar playing and lyrics were mesmerizing. I couldn't believe this was the guy who wrote these songs. The guitar was passed around the room and other singers sang Hank Williams tunes or ones they had recently written. At the end of the evening Willie invited me to come see him play and sit in with his band.

Well, this piqued my interest.

Several months later I heard that Willie was playing a benefit in Lancaster, Texas, for a volunteer fire department. I drove down from Dallas with my little box of harmonicas and showed up at his bus and asked if the offer still stood to sit in with his band.

He very graciously invited me to play. As a novice at country music, I was lost and struggled to keep up, faking it the whole time. I think by the fourth time we played "Fräulein" I was getting the hang of it.

Willie had left Nashville and moved to Austin,

where the music scene was exploding. Long-haired hippie types (my peers) were mingling with rednecks, and what brought them together was music. Willie saw this was happening and found a new home in Austin.

Willie and the band would travel in this camper called an Open Road, like a Winnebago, but it only had a screen door in front, which really made it an "Open Road."

After I played with Willie for several weekends, Willie asked Paul English, his drummer and bandleader, "What are we paying Mickey?" Paul told Will, "We're paying him nothing; he's just coming around on his own."

Willie's response was "Double his salary."

This was 1973 and it's 2012 now.

Life never gets dull out here. Every day is an adventure and some days are harder than others, but it beats a real job. We just finished an outdoor gig in Las Vegas tonight, where it was 106 degrees onstage. The cooling fans onstage were blowing and Willie thought a heater was on because the blowing air was so hot. He just kept playing and gave them his all.

When I started this gig, I was twenty-one and I'm sixty now. I learned so much from watching Willie play, and his unique phrasing has given me a musical education I would have received nowhere else.

It's been an amazing ride, and I'm thankful every day for the call I got from Darrell and Edith Royal. I'm even more grateful Willie took their advice and took a chance on me.

Willie has been a friend, a brother, a father, a boss, a benevolent dictator, a sometimes crazy motherfucker, and a great inspiration to me.

I grew up in this band of heathens and I'm thankful to be a foster child in this family.

MARK ROTHBAUM, JOEL KATZ, AND LARRY GOLDFEIN STILL TAKE care of most all my music business, and they are all very good. Mark Rothbaum is my manager, even though I hesitate to say he's my "manager," mostly because I'm not very manageable. But he represents me very well and helps me make decisions. Joel Katz is a great music lawyer; we kid him a lot and tell him his favorite song is "Both Sides Now." Brian Greenbaum is my booking agent with CAA. He books my tours and does a great job. Larry Goldfein is a great tax lawyer and saved my ass big-time when the IRS stuff was all going on, but that's another book.

If you don't get their money at least get some advice, because they know a lot. For them I wrote, "Why Do I Have Two Jews?" . . . or was that "Why Do I Have to Choose?" I can't remember, but now you know why . . . because I couldn't do it without them! They have done a remarkable job representing me, so thank you, gentlemen!

MARK ROTHBAUM

When you wholeheartedly adopt a "with all your heart" attitude, and go out with positive principle, you can do incredible things.

—Dr. Norman Vincent Peale

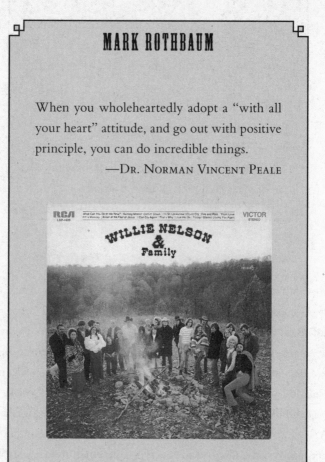

The album *Willie Nelson and Family* was released in 1971. The cover was a photograph of all the members of the band, along with their families, posed around a campfire. The first time I saw that picture was in 1973. There is Willie, the patriarch, proud, strong, focused—a man on a mission. His wife, kids, friends, and bandmates surround him. At one end, Bobbie, looking so beautiful and proper. At the other end, Paul "the Devil" English, wearing red pants and a red cape, looking just insane enough to be feared, but adorable just the same. Standing around the fire were Bee, Lana, Susie, Billy, P.C., and many others. . . . I wanted to be a part of that circle.

Mark Rothbaum

I was working for a management company in New York City that represented musicians, in particular Waylon Jennings, Willie Nelson, and Miles Davis, who, as a matter of fact, got me the job. I was responsible for the day-to-day needs of Miles. I was twenty-four years old and had no music business experience, but I kept going back to that photo, and of course, the music. I was now completely head over heels into Willie Nelson.

When the company needed someone to represent Willie, they did not think of me. I had no desk and no phone. I had no responsibility other than Miles's daily needs. Soon a music industry veteran was given the huge sum of $5,000 to come in and take over Willie's day-to-day management. This guy was supposed to show up on Monday morning; in fact, he showed up after lunch! He was a mess. His hair was all disheveled, and sleep was in his eyes. It hit me all at once: positive thinking! I could run this guy into the ground. Why couldn't I manage Willie Nelson? Why couldn't I be a part of that circle? I was positive I could be a great manager.

As a kid, I would make deliveries for my dad's furniture store and get $75 a week in return. Right away I would run out to buy albums with that money. He would always say to me, "What can you do with that music? How can you make a living with just music?" I always loved music. For as far back as I can remember, great songs were part of my life.

Now I had the opportunity to do what I loved, and I wasn't going to let it get away from me. Everything crystallized at once. I began to study concert, television, and record-company contracts. I was paying attention to details. When the phone rang, I was the first one to answer it. For each question I asked, I continued to have more swirling through my head. About a month later, I had a desk and a

AS I MENTIONED BEFORE, WE LOST THE BEE MAN. BEE SPEARS WAS A
great bass player and all-around fantastic human being. He is still
missed all the time.

Kevin Smith has jumped in on bass and is doing a great job! It's
not easy to follow Bee, and playing with us is a lot of ESP that takes
time to master. I never know what I'm going to do, so of course
the band is never sure either. It's kind of like walking the high wire
with no net. There are no take twos in a live show, and you can't
take nothin' back, so the best way to follow me onstage is really
simple: you wait, wait, and then wait some more until you know
what I am doing, then jump in. If you are a good musician you will
know what to do.

Wynton Marsalis told me a story about a jazz musician who
asked the bandleader who had just hired him, "When do we rehearse?" The bandleader said, "Can you play?" The musician said,
"Well, yes." The bandleader said, "Well then, what the fuck do you
want to rehearse for?" It makes sense that either you can play or
you can't play. It's too late to learn once you get out there. You turn

everything over to your inner self and go for it. You have to trust yourself, and that requires confidence and talent.

THE SOUND DEPARTMENT IS BOBBY LEMONS AND AARON FOYE. The lighting department is Budrock Pruitt. They do a great job of making us look and sound good. John Selman is the stage manager. He makes sure everything is perfect for the shows each and every night. Kenny Keopke works with John to keep the show going. Tom Hawkins has been wrangling Trigger for me for many years now. I know that at showtime Trigger will be tuned and ready to bark. Larry "L.G." Gorham has been watching my back for over thirty years. Gates "Gator" Moore and Tony Sizemore have been driving the bus for me for millions of miles. We have worn out several buses, and when we all lie down to sleep, we know that our lives are as safe as they can be. Thank you, Gator and Tony; we are here because you got us here. David Anderson is maybe the smartest guy I have out there, besides Paul. He does everything he has to do very well—public relations, road manager, computer wizard, and sparring partner. I practiced all my tae kwon do forms on the bus, going down the road at sixty miles an hour, using David as my opponent. He was a good sport. Thank you all very much!

DAVID ANDERSON

It was New Year's Eve 1973, after my senior high school party; I was high on mushrooms and riding up and down on the Dallas Hyatt Regency elevator for fun. It was there I experienced my first encounter with the man I would spend the rest of my adult life with. A man who would change—had already changed—my life forever.

Shortly after midnight, the elevator door opened and through the hallucinogenic glaze of my eyes stood before me one of the largest super-stars in history, and next to him was Willie Nelson. I offered Leon Russell and Willie a ride, asked them what floor they wanted, and delivered them safe and sound with great relief. My journalism and sociology teachers had recently introduced me to Willie's music while trying to explain why Leon Russell had just cut his first country record, *Hank Wilson's Back*.

That next year, our paths would cross yet again. It was during a very new growth period for Texas music and music festivals in general. Tom Lett, owner of the Best Parking Lot at Dallas's Love Field, had the pioneering idea of bringing festivals to the heart of Dallas during the pre-amphitheater era. I was an eighteen-year-old kid right out of film school and enjoyed music, though I was far from an expert. But when the chance came along for me to advise Tom on the artists who should perform, I jumped at the chance.

Willie was my first choice, and Willie's daugh-ter Lana was my first call. She worked in her dad's office, booking and helping Paul English, Willie's drummer. She's now my big sister and best friend.

Tickets were $7 each and included all the beer

and soda you could consume. They sold out instantly. We built the stage on top of the parking lot entrance, and that night two topless girls climbed onto two other cowboys' shoulders to see Willie up close and personal. Willie enjoyed the view until the blonde fell and grabbed on to Willie's strap. It was an eighteen-foot fall and no titties were worth the drop.

Fate continued to guide me as I opted out of a consulting fee and salary, and I asked Tom to rent me a suite at the Ramada Inn next door with a banquet room for the artists to come to and relax and party instead. Much better, I thought, than a hundred-dollar bill. Willie, Paul, and the rest of the band came up for food and to smoke a quick joint, and of course to get paid, before hitting the road. We did, they did, and it was done.

Later on, while Paul was producing the 1975 picnic in Liberty Hill, he stayed in Dallas to promote and buy ads, although it turned out to be a retreat from exhaustion more than anything. We met each night after my job at Bill Stokes's studio and talked about the picnic, exchanging ideas on how to make it work easier than in the past.

It was their fourth year and most motor-home rental agencies had seen the wrath of a picnic taken out on their equipment, and they had all refused to rent to them, a conundrum Paul placed on my shoulders. With the arrogance of naïveté, I jumped at the chance. I didn't even know what a dressing room was, much less where to rent one.

The next Sunday I was driving by a construction site and fifty blueprint office trailers were scattered around a field. I called the number on the billboard and ordered them all delivered to Austin for $50 each. Before I knew it, I was in Austin at another picnic, only this time not as a spectator, but as a worker helping "the Devil" himself.

It rained that year, as it seems to at most picnics, and the roof began filling with water and had nowhere to go, so Paul pulled out his forty-five and unloaded his pistol into it to drain the weight of the water. Like the rest of the audience I cheered on in happy disbelief. I'd never seen a gun before.

I guess he was enthused over my eagerness, because Paul hired me as his assistant. Willie's enthusiasm, however, was short-lived. I was getting on his nerves, trying to treat him like the star I thought he was.

Soon Willie called me into his office. Paul was there too, and in true Willie fashion, rather than hurt my feelings, he said he couldn't afford to pay me. I knew that wasn't the case, as I had worked the last nine months for only $100.

He did say, however, that I could continue to promote shows for him, so I did just that. Wichita Falls was my first true dive into the world of concert promotion, and with Willie as the headliner it was an easy sell. The show sold out with massive profits for the time, $12,500; I had about $6,500 in cash sales, with the other $6,000 at the box office.

Fate decided to take me on a drive out west to deliver the money. Paul and Willie were at a show promoted by a longtime scoundrel, Geno McCoslin. Geno had not paid them, yet again, and to their surprise and my good fortune, I showed up with a brown paper bag with $6,500 cash. Willie told Paul, "Hire him back."

It's been the best and worst times of my life. I couldn't imagine a better person with whom to have experienced almost four decades of the most fascinating life anyone could ever imagine. He taught me all about love and how to love others. Just as Joe Jamail wrote on Trigger years ago, he's "a gentle man." I will always love him.

THE FRANKS BROTHERS HANDLE THE MERCHANDISE ON THE ROAD. Scooter, Ruthie, and crew travel every mile we do. They are the only merchandise company I have ever used.

OH WELL, HERE TODAY AND OUT THE OTHER . . . OR IN ONE EAR AND gone tomorrow. We live and learn, then die and forget it all. Maybe not, and maybe Earth is a school where we come to learn lessons. I believe in the law of karma, where every action has an equal and opposite reaction. You get what you give. Fred Foster said, "The only thing you get to keep in this life is what you gave away." You can't out-give God. The Bible says whatever you give away you get back ten times over. Do the math; it's a no-brainer, and I believe you keep coming back until you get it right. As you learn, you can also teach others what you have learned along the way. Or you can keep doing it wrong until you like it that way. So get to giving, and let me know how it works out. I have received more than ten times what I gave, and I'm still way ahead.

I GUESS I'VE COME TO LIVE HERE IN YOUR EYES

I guess I've come to live here in your eyes
This must be the place called paradise
You are so special to me
And what a precious time within our lives
And I guess I've come to live here in your eyes

A thousand times I see you and a thousand times you take my
*   breath away*
Then fears and doubts consume me
I'm afraid someone will take it all away
I hope I'm here forever, but I think it's time that we both realize
That I guess I've come to live here in your eyes

ANNIE AND I HAVE BEEN TOGETHER ALMOST TWENTY-SEVEN YEARS and have been married for nearly twenty-two of those. Do the math yourself if you like, or I can just tell you that both of our boys were in our wedding.

73

Micah and Lukas

We seem to still find ways and time to be together. We have two great sons, Lukas and Micah, who are fantastic musicians, singers, and artists. They always make me so proud. When I'm really lucky, we all get together onstage and play music. Playing music with Paula, Amy, Lukas, Micah, and Sister Bobbie is as good as it gets!

MICAH NELSON

For those who still believe Santa Claus isn't real, clearly they have never met my father. The invaluable things I have learned from him over the years simply through observation are more than I can describe in any language. It is a blessing to have been raised by someone so wise and humble. He is an elder of the human tribe and young beyond his years. I love him more every day, because every day it seems we grow closer.

It isn't easy to describe exactly what it's like to be "Willie's kid." One might reasonably assume that it comes with a great pressure to live up to a certain expectation or to be caught in a heavy shadow. Being an artist/musician inherently comes with many pressures and struggles. However, I have never felt as though I am standing in his shadow—it is instead as if he has blazed a trail of lights for me with which to cast my own shadows. There has never been any pressure from him to be anything but a decent person, and he has supported me in every creative endeavor I've ever embarked upon, regardless of how different it may be. Seriously, even if I played in some screamo/breakcore/noise/glitch pop/polka band (fill in the blank), he would still want to come sit in with the band or have me come open for him or something, just so we could hang out and play music together. That is how much he cares about family above all else. When he came to see my band Insects vs. Robots a couple years ago, our bassist broke a string halfway through the set, and while he was changing it, my dad jumped onstage and kicked off "On the Road Again." Maybe half the band knew the song, but it kept the show moving and was a great and hilarious moment. I'll never forget that.

I started playing harmonica in his band next to Mickey when I was three years old and later moved on to playing drums/percussion with Paul and Billy, while Lukas played guitar, and these days I've been singing in the band as well. I literally grew up with music. When I was about seven years old, Dad asked me to make the album artwork for his album *Milk Cow Blues*. I ended up giving the "boy cows" udders (because I was seven years old), but he didn't care. In fact, he thought it was great. For us, it was just a fun project to do together.

When he asked me to do illustrations for this book, it was just another great excuse to create together. Still, I feel incredibly honored to be the one to illustrate moments and characters in my dad's life. It has certainly been a special one. Needless

Lukas, Micah, and Willie

to say, we laughed a lot rummaging through all his life stories. Getting to re-create them visually has made us closer than ever. When I originally asked what he had in mind visually for the book he said, "Just do what you do, whatever you're feeling. We'll go from there." My dad has never tried to hinder my creative potential or change who I am, and for that I thank him so much. He's had his fair share of experience being himself in the face of creative suppression and trusting his intuition regardless of what was expected or accepted. Seems to have worked out pretty well so far.

THEY SAY THERE ARE NO EX-WIVES, ONLY ADDITIONAL WIVES, AND that's not such a bad thing, especially if you had kids together. It's good to stay on good terms with everyone.

My first wife, Martha, was a great lady. We were just teenagers when we met. She was a carhop in Waco, and I was a guitar player. We had three great kids, Lana, Susie, and Billy. We lost Billy, and that's still hard to think about. You never get over losing a child, you only get through it. Lana travels with me on the road now. Susie lives in Austin. She is doing a radio show on SiriusXM playing gospel music.

Susie, Billy, Martha, and Lana

RAELYN NELSON

So, Annie told me she needs this yesterday; that gives me until tomorrow afternoon to ponder and write about Papa Willie memories and such. The earliest memory I have of Papa Willie (I've always called him Papa Willie until I shortened it to PW, then eventually to P-dub) is with my daddy. I remember just a flash, as early memories are for most of us, of my daddy, P-dub, and me singing a song. I know it was "Jingle Bells," but only because I was told that was the song that they taught me. The other early memory I have is being in a crowded venue in my daddy's arms and watching P-dub try to make his way through hundreds of screaming fans. I wanted to talk to Papa Willie and my daddy told me we'd see him after he was done working.

My daddy was wild, hence the nickname Wild Bill. Auntie says, "Papa Willie must've never tamed him." That makes me smile. I remember my daddy always coming and going. When he was home with my mama and me, we'd play and have the best time. He left every few days, but he'd always come back ready to sing and play guitar to me and draw smiley faces. When he was gone, I always thought he was with P-dub, on the road. My daddy loved P-dub; I think he wanted to be just like him . . .

Billy

but who doesn't? It was hard being Willie Nelson Jr., I'm sure, and I'll never have the opportunity to talk to my dad about his struggles and tribulations of that time, but I know he was proud of his daddy. We'd go to every Papa Willie show we could make.

I was seven years old and it was Christmas Day when my mama got a call from Aunt Lana; my daddy had been found dead in his cabin in Ridgetop. My mama told me and I saw her cry. She cried hard, wept while my stepdad tried to console her. She took me to his memorial viewing in Tennessee, because she wanted me to see that he was dead and didn't just take off and hadn't come back yet.

My mama took me to all of P-dub's shows when he came through town, made sure I had all of his albums, had me call and write regularly, and did anything else she could to keep me connected with my daddy's family. I remember he came to Grand-parents' Day at my elementary school in fifth grade and signed autographs for everybody's grandparents for hours. I asked P-dub for a guitar when I was fourteen, and he bought me a brand-new Martin acoustic that I still play today. I learned some tunes, and the next time I saw him, I played and sang the best song I could play. He smiled and gave me a guitar lesson that I still hold as one of my most precious moments of life.

Whenever I see Papa Willie, there's a sadness in his eyes that I recognize, and I'm sure he

Raelyn and Papa Willie

sees it in mine, too, because just like I remind him of my daddy, he reminds me of my daddy, and the pain of losing him from this life never goes away. There's not a day that goes by that we don't think about him. He's still alive in our hearts and minds and I believe that he's watching over us as a family angel . . . so don't fuck with us.

MARTHA AND I STAYED TOGETHER TEN YEARS BEFORE MY SHENANI- gans on the road blew the deal. She is no longer with us, but we had some great years. Our marriage got a little rocky when I met Shirley Collie. Shirley was a great singer and songwriter. We stayed together ten years before I met this real pretty blonde in Texas one night, and there I went again.

Connie and I stayed together ten years, and we had two great kids, Amy and Paula. I began to see a pattern.

AND SO WILL YOU MY LOVE

The music stopped the crowd is thinning now
One phase of night has reached an ending now
But nothing, nothing lasts forever
Except forever
And you my love
And so will you my love, my love

The streets are dark here as I walk alone
And since you're gone I always walk alone
But nothing, nothing lasts forever
Except forever and you my love
And so will you my love, my love

And so will you my love
Your memory is always near

Wherever I am found your memory's still around

The dawn and I arrive at home at last
Night turns its lonely face toward the past
For nothing lasts forever
Except forever

And you my love
And so will you my love
My
Love

THEN I DID A MOVIE IN TUCSON AND MET ANNIE. SHE WAS THE makeup artist on the movie *Stagecoach*. We have been together almost twenty-seven years, so we seem to have figured it out . . . as much as anyone can. I still travel a lot, but we still find our time. They say the only normal family is the one you don't really know, so I guess we are as normal as the next. I think somebody said we get too soon old and too late smart, and why is youth wasted on the young?

ANNIE NELSON

When I'm out on the road, most people ask how Willie and I met. I met Willie on a "movie of the week" filming in Tucson, Arizona. The film was a remake of John Ford's classic *Stagecoach*. I actually met the rest of the highwaymen and their families before I met the guy who turned out to be my favorite—oh wait, my only—husband.

I was the head of the hair and makeup department for the film and had spent an inordinate amount of time going back and forth with the director and producer, who felt that Willie should cut his hair to play the part of John Henry "Doc" Holliday. I know what you're thinking. Why? Because

I was thinking the same thing myself. I agreed finally that I would go ahead and do it. So the first day he showed up, my job was to ask Willie Nelson if he would be willing to cut his lovely hair off to play the part of a character who, in truth, didn't really have long hair. In any case, I introduced myself to him and said, "Mr. Nelson, the producers would like to know if you are willing to cut your hair off for this part." He was sitting, so he looked up at me with an impish grin and said, "What do you think?" Now, honestly, I was willing to leave the show at that point because I had already spent a few days listening to the producer and director fighting via bullhorns across the desert Southwest over who had worked on the most John Wayne films. I was pretty done. So it was easy to say to him, "I think it is spectacularly unnecessary and ridiculous." That's when his impish grin grew to a fantastic smile and a twinkle in his eye, and he said, "Then let's say no!" That's the moment I saw my home in his eyes. Maybe it was just a shared moment of smart-assedness, but it's been going strong for nearly twenty-seven years, so I guess there was something there after all.

After that, it was all just life happening, and working out how I was going to give up my career because whenever he was off on a tour, I was somewhere else on the planet working on a film, and something had to give for us to be together. Obviously we worked it out.

"And when you get right down to it, there it is."
I think Zeke Varner said that.

Annie and I are flying back to Maui now. I just finished a great tour. We had good crowds and played well. You can't ask for anything better than that, and I can't either.

Maui is kind of like a hospital zone for me. It has healing qualities, like the sun and aloha mixed together. It is good medicine. Annie and I love coming here, and we do every chance we get. Annie loves to cook—she's a really a great chef and keeps getting better. She loves to invite the island over and feed them all. That is her hobby.

Me, I love to gamble with my friends (surprise, surprise). My friend Zeke was good at poker and dominoes. He taught me a lot. I love to invite my gambling buddies over and see who's the luckiest son of a gun tonight.

Maui

• • •

THINK IT AND BE IT, AND YEA THOUGH I WALK THROUGH THE VALLEY of the shadow of death, I will fear no evil, because I'm the meanest son of a bitch in the valley. Do you think that I am a little over-confident? Maybe, but I believe the best defense is a great offense, and whoever lands the first blow has the advantage. Like Billy Joe Shaver said, "I don't start fights, but I try really hard to finish them."

I've been beaten up a few times, and I never learned to like it. If I can scare you off with big talk, I'll try that first. Hide grows back, but good clothes don't, and in the early days I didn't have a lot of clothes. Speaking of Billy Joe Shaver, he is one of the best songwriters, alive or dead. He is in the same league as Kris Kristof-ferson, Hank Williams, Merle Haggard, Vern Gosdin, or anybody. He says it like it is with as few words as possible, and that's the real formula, I think.

I sing Billy Joe Shaver's song "Georgia on a Fast Train" and Waylon Jennings's "You Ask Me To" every night, because they are great songs.

One time Billy Joe was in one of the shows I put on in Austin, Texas. It was in a cow pasture in Dripping Springs. He took some peyote before he got there and thought he was Jesus. He preached for hours to anyone who would listen. He said he saved a lot of souls that day and baptized them in a mud puddle. They were very grate-ful, and still love the lord till this day as far as I know.

Kris and I have been great friends forever. Kris is still writing great songs. I did an album of Kris's songs and an album of Billy Joe's songs. I still sing "Help Me Make It Through the Night," "Loving Her Was Easier," and "Me and Bobby McGee" in my shows. We played music and acted in movies together, like *Songwriter*. We also made a Western in Spain that I really enjoyed. We got to ride horses and play music with Gypsies every night. That's hard to beat.

Thought for the Day: If there is no solution, then there is no problem.

These are words to live by, you should teach them to your kids, and if there is one thing I know for sure, it's I don't know nothin' for sure. I think I'm smart . . . start with that one.

ANNIE NELSON

Besides my own father, my husband is one of the funniest people I know, and the very best person I have ever met. It is true that after years together you get set in your ways and can finish each other's thoughts before you've even had them, which might seem mundane to some, but the one thing that lasts is a sense of humor. Our family will always be fine because if anything gets too heavy, one of us cracks a joke, and every one of us appreciates the humor (translated: we are all smart-asses), so the heavy just disappears. I highly recommend humor for relationship longevity. It's hard to stay mad when you're laughing your ass off.

With kids, the sense of humor really comes in handy. When Lukas was born, I was having a hard time with the lack of privacy. I wanted the time, after both the boys' births, for my family to bond alone. Turns out you can get that time, but boy, do you have to be a bitch to make it happen. It did happen, however (ergo some bitch was had), and both boys are completely bonded with their father. I believe that bond is due to the time we got alone, and the fact that when they were young we took them everywhere with us. Both Lukas and Micah learned to walk on the bus, which I believe is one reason sports like surfing that stress strong balance were easy for them.

We taught them to use their words to express their feelings, and that's what you really need to have a sense of humor about. But when you are a parent, your words coming back at you can some-times be something you absolutely have to learn to laugh about!

I HOUSEBROKE MY DOG. EVERY TIME HE SHIT ON THE FLOOR I WOULD rub his nose in it, then throw him out the window. Now when he shits on the floor, he rubs his nose in it and jumps right out the window.

INTERMISSION

I shouldn't have a problem writing this book; I'm so opinionated that I can give you my opinion on anything, anytime, and I'm glad to do it because I'm just an asshole. But they say opinions are like assholes: everybody has one. I guess. "While in all your knowing, know yourself first." I'm not sure who said that. It was either Billy Joe Shaver or Jesus.

GOLF

Swing hard, you might hit it. That was my first idea about golf, and learning to swing *easy* is still a work in progress. Mark Twain said, "Golf is a good walk spoiled." I own a golf course and recording studio outside of Austin at the Pedernales Cut-N-Putt in Spicewood, Texas. The great writer-producer Chips Moman built the music studio, which sits next to the golf course. We cut "Pancho and Lefty" and "Always on My Mind" there, and I still record there.

Sister Bobbie and I just did some recording there. Buddy brought all the good pickers in Nashville down to record my new CD *Heroes* at the Pedernales Cut-N-Putt. My son Lukas is singing with me on the new CD as well. He is so good, it's scary, and when Micah is there painting, singing, and playing, it all sure makes a great picture.

LUKAS NELSON

My dad has been a perfect example of the type of father I hope to be one day. He has shown me, with and without words, how to conduct myself with grace in the world. That is, in my opinion, the best form of teaching. I have always wanted to be like my father because people enjoy being around him and feel comfortable in his presence. What more can we ask for in the bettering of ourselves? Not perfection, that's for sure. It is ease that he exemplifies. Ease of mind, ease of heart . . . I see him make mistakes, and I watch them dissolve into lessons effortlessly for him. This is what I have learned from him. I have learned how to find the ease in most every situation. It is the most valuable tool that I have in my life and has allowed me to quiet my mind enough to follow my bliss.

HIGHWAYMEN

I met Waylon Jennings one night in Phoenix, Arizona, at an all-night restaurant next to the Holiday Inn where I was staying. We hit it off pretty good right from the start. We were both from Texas and were already called "outlaws." I don't know about Waylon, but I ate it up. It was good for my image. Waylon asked me if I thought

Waylon Jennings

he should go to Nashville. I asked him how much money he was making in Phoenix, and he said four hundred a week. I told him to stay where he was. I was getting like five hundred a night, but the commissions, hotel, fuel, food, and traveling took it all. I thought he had a better gig than I did. Fortunately, he didn't listen to me.

We stayed great friends all the way. We disagreed on almost everything and argued like old married people. We were on different drugs. He liked speed, and I didn't like speed. I was going too fast already.

The Highwaymen tours were the most fun I ever had before or since. Kris and Waylon would argue about politics; John and I would laugh a lot. Later on they would call me just to hear a good joke. I loved John and Waylon. They are dearly missed to this day.

Kris and his wife, Lisa, came by this week on his way to somewhere. He looked great. We laughed a lot, burned one down, and solved all the world's problems. I love you, Kris; you're the real deal!

ANNIE NELSON

All the Highwaymen tours were probably my most relaxing and fun tour times. We had four full families on giant tours, all over the planet. Our kids all pretty much grew up on the road. It was the Nelson, Kristofferson, Jennings, and Cash gang all growing up and seeing the world together. Lisa Kristofferson and I were pregnant together at one point, and one of my favorite memories of those times was June Carter Cash telling us both not to worry while we were out there because if either of us went into labor, she was there to deliver them babies! She would have done it too. I loved June and miss her to this day. Our boys were not spoiled with material possessions, but they were spoiled with experience. They traveled all over the planet, and when we were in other countries, they played in parks with other children and never had to share a language, just the fact that they were children; the language of children was the only one they needed to know. They learned so much sharing those times. Knowing people from other cultures gave them the gift of understanding that we really are all the same, and no matter how different we may look, or how ideologically apart we are, we really have more in common than not. We all love, laugh, cry, and are moved by the common language of music together. I am so grateful that I chose the husband I did, so that our children would be children of the world and contributors to the common good.

It is amazing to see those little kids who grew up on the road, now all playing music together. A couple of months ago, John Carter Cash, June and Johnny Cash's son and part of the "HighwayKid posse," produced a Johnny Cash birthday concert. The whole show was so emotional for me. Many of the musicians onstage were also musicians on some of the Highwaymen tours. When they started playing the song "The Highwayman," that was it; I lost it! Onstage were Willie, Kris, Shooter Jennings (standing up for his father), and Jamey Johnson. When Willie and Kris started into their parts of the song, it was as if twenty-five years simply melted away. It was a moment that took me back, and I could see the four of them singing together and cracking each other up.

When the kids were little, they would be on the side of the stage, always dancing and singing along with their dads. On the Johnny Cash birthday night, Lukas was on the road touring with his band the Promise of the Real, but Micah was there onstage playing the charango along with the band! The times they do change, but the road maybe does go on forever, and the party just may never end!

Willie and Kris Kristofferson

It must be true that as you get older the more you look like your pet, because my neighbor came over this morning and chewed me out for shitting in his front yard.

—ROGER MILLER

Roger Miller was the funniest son of a bitch in the world. He kept me laughing for years. Here are a few Roger jokes:

A lady had bought a screen door at a hardware store. As she was leaving the clerk said, "Do you want a screw for that?" She said, "No, but I'll blow you for that toaster."

musician. She is so talented in so many other ways, like writing, art, and making videos, and she has a great sense of humor. She can turn trash into a thing of beauty. I'm lucky to have her on the bus with me.

LANA NELSON

It is an honor and a privilege to be the Flighty Attendant aboard the *Honeysuckle Rose* tour bus. I hate to call it a bus; it's actually more of a member of the family than a bus. More time will be spent wrapped in these steel arms than anywhere else in the world. It's a dear friend that's also a home. Some days it's just a handful of us onboard, leisurely traveling across America the beautiful, but other times we are packed so tight folks are sleeping on the floors. Every day is a different challenge. I will be serving, cooking, cleaning, and assisting with luggage and various secretarial chores. My duties may change daily, but my desire to be there doesn't.

All I have ever wanted to be or do was to work with Dad and help him with his career, to be his head cheerleader. I would listen to his radio shows when he was a local DJ and I was a toddler. My favorite song was "Redheaded Stranger," a song by Arthur Smith that he would play on his noon radio show. He would sing it to me at night to put me to sleep and he promised someday he would record it so I could listen to it whenever I wanted to.

I cried when he sold his song "Family Bible" because I thought no one would ever know how talented he was if his name wasn't on the record. Dad was sweet and explained to me how we really needed the fifty dollars and everything would be okay. He made another promise: that someday he would buy us enough land to stretch as far as we can see and none of the events of today would even matter anymore. I was four years old.

When I was a kid, we moved a lot—every time the rent came due—and I was always trying to make new friends. I'd wind up having to explain how my daddy worked in the daytime *and* at night because he was a musician and that's just what they do, and how making saddles or selling vacuum cleaners wasn't his real talent but rather just a way for him to make money. He was actually a big star. I'd give them a quick rundown on some of the songs he had written and how someday they would be huge hits and they could say they knew him when.

I never went as far as my cousins Randy, Mike, and Freddie. They set up tours through Aunt Bobbie's house and into the room where Dad was sleeping, granting the other kids in the neighborhood a quick glimpse of a rising star for twenty-five cents.

Dad nearly gave his life for me in a shoot-out with my abusive first husband, Steve, and then wrote the song "Shotgun Willie" about the whole ordeal. I have always liked the way he copes with disaster.

In 1975 Dad hired me away from the state of Texas and a job at the state capitol to be his secretary at a little office we had in Oak Hill west of Austin. I paid some of his bills and wrote the checks, including the ones to the band, which was then on a $225 weekly retainer to keep everyone from either starving or getting another job. We moved the offices to a house in Dripping Springs that Dad and Connie had just left empty after they moved to Colorado. It was out of this house that we promoted various other concerts and the Fourth of July picnic in Liberty Hill. You know that one. That's the picnic where Paul whipped out his gun and shot holes in the sagging roof of the stage to relieve the intense water pressure from that afternoon's torrential rains. It wasn't the only time that day that Paul used his gun, but it was the most productive.

When Mark became Dad's manager, we moved the main offices to Danbury, Connecticut. Soon afterward Dad bought the Pedernales Golf Club, plus seven hundred acres nearby. We turned the clubhouse into the Pedernales Cut-N-Putt recording studio (which I managed). At the time the golf course was private for his friends, family, and musicians who were recording at the Cut-N-Putt.

We built a western town on the seven hundred acres for a movie Dad produced, based on his No. 1 hit album *Red Headed Stranger.* I had never even been on a movie set when Dad and Bill Wittliff (the movie's director) asked me to be the costume designer. I did, and surprisingly enough the costumes drew some good reviews. We were all flying by the seat of our panties on that one, but we pulled it off. We had our movie.

Somewhere during those years I directed his music videos for "Pancho and Lefty," "Tougher Than Leather," and "There You Are." "Pancho and Lefty" won an American Video Award for best country video, and "Tougher Than Leather" was nominated a couple of years later. I can say that proudly; we lost to Ray Charles. Most recently David Anderson and I wrote and directed Dad's next music video, "A Horse Called Music," due out this fall.

CAROLYN MUGAR

We were filming the movie *Red Headed Stranger* in Austin, Texas. The studio offered to film it with an $18 million budget and Robert

Redford as the lead, which was my part of the preacher. I decided to pass, not because I didn't like Robert Redford—in fact we are friends to this day and I love the man. I passed because it was a part I really wanted to play. I asked my friend and director Bill Wittliff if we could do it for less. We settled on a $1.8 million budget and began to raise our own money. Don Tyson (of Tyson Foods) gave us the first $250,000 to get started and a few more friends here and there came up with $25,000 and $50,000 investments. It was far from enough to finish the film but enough for me to say, "Let's go for it." I had already built, and paid for, a huge film town on my property, so we just started filming. We invited Cheryl McCall, a writer for *Life* magazine and a dear friend, to embed herself and the magazine in our production set and gave them total access. She would often just hang out with me between takes. One day while we were filming on Bill's ranch outside of Austin, my tour manager David Anderson, who helped coproduce the movie and kept the books, came to the set to talk money. After delivering the bad news that we were more than $150,000 overdrawn and hadn't finished the first weeks of production, Cheryl interrupted and said that a friend she knew was having dinner with a woman from Boston, and she had money that she might be willing to invest. David was far from moved by the idea and was rude as usual—even though, in his defense, it did seem like quite a stretch.

The next morning, the mysterious woman from Boston showed up with $500,000, and that was how I met one of my closest confidants, Carolyn Mugar. It turns out we had a great deal in common, and she is still my friend to this day.

MARCH 2012

We just put Luke on a plane to Los Angeles. He has gigs to play up and down the coast, and then he goes to NYC to do the Letterman show, ho-hum. He has every right to be a spoiled little—I mean big—brat. But he is not. He has a really good heart and loves everyone; he gets that from his mom.

ANNIE NELSON

While raising our boys, I pretty much considered myself a married single parent. Don't get me wrong, I have the best husband in the world, but he was gone a lot, and when we weren't with him, I was on my own. People ask me, "How do you do it?" but the truth is we both love it. I think one of the secrets to our longevity is the fact that we are basically both gypsies in our souls, so traveling is in my bones, and I am okay on my own—in fact, I enjoy it. I am excited to see him when he comes home, and about the time he's got to go and is ready to go . . . he's really got to go! The trick, I think, is that he feels the same way. Willie is always happy to come home and to have time off, but if he's off too long he starts to go through "picker's withdrawal" and needs to play music somewhere—anywhere!

TODAY IS THURSDAY, MARCH 24, 2012

These dates are more for me than for you. It's good for me to know what month, year, date, and time of day it is, and oh yeah . . . where I am.

"Beautiful" is not a good enough word for Maui. It is breathtaking, healing, addictive, and a lot of other wonderful descriptions, and I still haven't completely described Maui. I have lived here many years, and in some ways it reminds me of Abbott, Texas, my hometown. Paia, Maui, Hawaii, is a great place.

Annie is in the house cooking up a storm with Woody's wife, Laura, and a bunch of our kids. It's nice to have extended family here, or as we call it, the Tribe. We even have a room in the house called the Woody Wing. When he's winning, he goes home; when he's losing, the Woody Wing is occupied.

Now it's poker time. Six twenty-two P.M., also known as "dark thirty."

IT'S 7:13 P.M., SATURDAY, APRIL FOOL'S DAY

Don't believe a word I say from here on. Just kidding. Trying to get this day started; it ain't easy. Maybe I'll go back to sleep and try again later.

APRIL 2012

Annie and I head to Los Angeles tonight. It ain't easy leaving heaven on earth, aka Maui, Hawaii. I start playing on the fifth in Texas. That will be good, because I'm ready for a great Texas crowd. Texas crowds get into it pretty good, and I love it when they do. The people put on as good a show as we do, and I feel the vibes. We send out good ones and they send them right back.

That means it all worked out right.

Lukas, Micah, Annie, and me

WHEREVER YOU ARE RIGHT NOW, SEND OUT SOME GOOD VIBES. Energy follows thought, and when you send it out, it keeps going. Every thought you have had is still spinning in the universe, so keep them positive. What goes around comes around, the law of karma—for every action there is an opposite and equal reaction, and I will keep saying this a lot, not for you, but for me. I need to hear it often. Earth is a school for dummies. We keep coming here to prove why we need to keep coming here. If we get it right just one time, I don't think we come back unless we just want to. Knowing what we know, I don't want to. It's too hard. Living is hard enough, dying really sucks, and I don't know, do the good times outweigh the bad? Fuck, I hope so.

GOOD TIMES

When I rolled rubber tires in the driveway
pulled a purse on a string across the highway
Classify these as good times good times

When I ran to the store with a penny
and when youth was abundant and plenty
Classify these as good times good times

Go to school fight a war working steady
Meet a girl fall in love before I'm ready
Classify these as good times good times

Here I sit with a drink and a memory
but I'm not cold I'm not wet and I'm not hungry
Classify these as good times good times
Good times are coming hum it um huh
Good times

FOR THOSE OF YOU WHO MIGHT BE OFFENDED BY MY BAD LANGUAGE, I do apologize. There are so few words that I want to be able to use them all if I can, cuss words too. The most holy word of all, God, cannot be used in vain if it is the most holy word. There is no way to say it in vain. When you say the word God, you vibrate at eighty-two billion times per second. That's why preachers say God and hold it a long time. It feels good to say it: GOOOOOOOOD. That's cool. God, good, it all means the same. It's the most powerful word in the English language—except for love. And God *is* love, so there you have it. Love is God, and God is love, end of story.

The first three letters in the universal language are "I am love," or "I am God," if you want to shake up the right a little. I am love, I am God, I am I, or if you think you feel bad, feel of me, or take your tongue out of my mouth, I'm kissing you good-bye, or I can't get over you so you get up and answer the phone, or I hate every bone in your body but mine, or take your love and stick it up your heart.

It's a nice plane ride. Nice plane, nice people taking care of you. That's nice. Thanks, American.

"Life is a bitch and then you die." Zeke really did say that.

There is a movie playing on the plane now, about people in a zoo of some kind. The star is very popular. I can't think of his name, but he went down with the Titanic. *I met him once at a fund-raiser . . . hmm. Oh well. I had a friend who went down on an elevator and another one who blew a safe, but that's another story. Was it Leonardo da Vinci? Maybe, I don't know . . . DiCaprio! He's a good actor, and I'm so proud of me for remembering his name. Oh yeah, that Da Vinci guy is a painter. Now I remember; I think he painted* The Last Supper.

• • •

ONE TIME A GUY COMMISSIONED A PAINTER TO PAINT A PICTURE THAT would show what General Custer was thinking at the Battle of Little Bighorn—that would actually *show his last thought*. When he was through, he had painted a picture of a thousand Indians lying on the ground having sex, and a cow with a halo. The financier asked, "What does this have to do with General Custer's last thoughts at the Battle of Little Bighorn?" The artist pointed to the caption on the painting, which read: "Holy cow, look at them fucking Indians."

I am part Cherokee, on my mother's side. Of course when she was in Texas she claimed to be Mexican, so I'm not really sure. My mother was a singer, guitar player, dancer, and bartender, and she did them all well. The first song I remember hearing her sing to me was "Ain't Nobody's Business."

> *Went downtown*
> *rode on a fender*
> *Came back home*
> *Kicked out a window*
> *Ain't nobody's business if I do*

I loved my mother. She also sang:

> *If you wanna get drunk and blow your top*
> *there ain't nobody gonna make you stop*
> *That's your red wagon*
> *That's your little red wagon*
> *That's your red wagon so just keep rolling along*

If you want to go fishing late at night
And you lose your bait and the fish don't bite
That's your red wagon and keep on rolling along

My mother, Myrle Greenhaw-Nelson, was a great cook. When we were in the northwest around Portland, Oregon, we would pull the bus up to the house and get the best meal we would have on the whole tour. We knew that and always looked forward to it. I was a DJ in Vancouver, Washington, and Portland, Oregon. I loved it. That's wonderful country, and I didn't mind the rain.

My dad, Ira Nelson, and my mother divorced when I was six months old and Sister Bobbie was three years old. I lived with my grandparents Nancy Elizabeth Nelson and William Alfred Nelson. My granddad was a blacksmith.

My dad moved to various places, following his trade as a mechanic. He made it a point to come visit every chance he could. Later on in life, we had more time to spend together. We played music all over the state together, and I was able to more than make up for the time I missed with him when I was a child. He tried to be a good father in every way.

He remarried a pretty lady called Lorraine. You may have heard stories about evil stepmothers, but Lorraine was *not* one of them. She loved me and Sister Bobbie, and coming into the family the way she did, "she had shit for a point," because in those days divorces and stepparents were hard to accept. Through the years, as we got to know her more and more, we realized what a great lady she was.

I LET MY MIND WANDER

I let my mind wander
And what did it do?
It just kept right on goin'
Until it got back to you
I let my mind wander

Can't trust it one minute
It's worse than a child
Disobeys without conscience
It's drivin' me wild
When I let my mind wander

Try to keep my mind busy
On thoughts of today
But invariably memories
Seem to lure it away

My lonely heart wonders
If there'll ever come a day
When I can be happy
But I can't see no way
'Cause I let my mind wander

I try to keep my mind busy
With thoughts of today
But invariably memories
Seem to lure it away

My lonely heart wonders
If there'll ever come a day
When I can be happy
But I can't see no way
'Cause I let my mind wander

SUMMERTIME

Summertime, and the livin' is easy

Oh wait, I didn't write that! Okay. Moving on.

DON NELSON HAS A POKER GAME NAMED AFTER HIM CALLED DIRTY Nellie. It is a dirty, unforgiving game. You get three cards—one up and two down—and your bottom hold card is wild. It's a seven-card game, so a lot can go wrong; I hate it. We play dealer's choice, and that can be one of a hundred games, like Spreckelsville; or a game I brought from Texas called Big Mountain or Omaha, where you play two cards only out of your hand; or Baldwin Beach, named after a local beach here and similar to Low Ball; or High Ball; or Paducah, and, honestly, more games than I can remember. Oh yes, and my favorite game is called Hold 'Em and Fuck 'Em. It's a five-card high/low game, hold card wild, buy one at the end, and throw one away. It's a great game. We play all kinds of games, crazy shit, but fun.

My good friend and one of the founding members out the Maui Outlaws, the late and great Spider, gave me a ship bell. We ring it for him every night at Django's Orchid Lounge. LIQUOR UP FRONT—POKER IN THE REAR.

Mudslide is a good friend who helps me keep Django's running. He sets up the poker table and brings coffee, beer, or whatever, to whomever. He plays and sings for us sometimes. He is a great entertainer and hard worker. He has worked every Farm Aid, helped park cars, buses, trucks, and whatever needs to be done. Slide can and will do it. Thank you, Slide.

Bill Mack and I have been great friends for fifty years at least. He was on the radio when I was just getting started, and he played all my records, from the first ones, like "Mr. Record Man," "Half a Man," and "Turn Out the Lights." He helped keep my name and music out there when I really needed it. He was the Midnight Cowboy at WBAP's Fort Worth, Texas, late-night show that everybody listened to.

In those days a radio station could make you or break you; I guess it still can. He was on SiriusXM Radio for years, and I believe he is coming back again. I sure hope so, anyway. We had a show on Wednesday together, called *Willie Wednesdays*. I hope we can do that again soon.

I JUST READ WHAT MELONIE CANNON WAS SAYING ABOUT THE 2012 CMA award show. It wasn't a good review, but it was a funny one! I didn't watch it, so I don't know for sure what went on, but it wasn't great according to Melonie. I think she was frustrated because she was raised on classic country music. I love Melonie and respect her opinion. She is a great singer and the daughter of one of the best writers, musicians, and producers in music, Buddy Cannon, so call 'em like you see 'em, Melonie.

PICKERS

I will not say anything bad about another picker, but we do know who the good ones are, and they were/are:

Django Reinhardt
Bob Wills
Ray Price
George Jones
Vern Gosdin
Kitty Wells
Loretta Lynn
Connie Smith
Little Jimmy Dickens
Floyd Tillman
Leon Payne
Ted Daffan
Spade Cooley
Tex Williams
Tennessee Ernie Ford
Chet Atkins
Grady Martin
Hank Garland
Tommy Jackson
Jerry Reed
Ernest Tubb

Red Foley
The Louvin Brothers
The Wilburn Brothers
Roy Acuff
Pee Wee King
Lulu Belle and Scotty
Marty Robbins
Waylon Jennings
Kris Kristofferson
Johnny Cash
Billy Joe Shaver
Merle Haggard
Hank Locklin
Carl Smith
Roger Miller
Carl and Pearl Butler
Jimmie Rodgers
Lefty Frizzell

These are some of the pickers who influenced me along the way, and I'm sure I am leaving somebody out, but these are the people I learned from, and whatever I am, I owe a lot to my teachers. Thank you for showing me the way.

IF YOU WANT TO BE A STAR, YOU SHOULD START ACTING LIKE ONE now, so that when you become one, you will already know how to behave, and maybe you won't blow it. For instance, I don't know anybody who is better drunk than sober. You might get by a while, but sooner than later it will take you down. I know. I tried it.

Nobody can stay drunk and make it for long. Alcohol and drugs will win. I have a high tolerance for pot, but I still forget "Whiskey River" if I smoke too much before a show. I don't drink anymore, so that's a plus, but I still have to watch it.

POT IS LEGAL IN A LOT OF PLACES AND ONE DAY WILL BE LEGAL EV-ERYwhere. If you make pot legal, and tax it and regulate it like alcohol and tobacco, you will stop the dealing on the borders and save thousands of lives!

THE NEXT SONG IS ON MY NEW RECORD. I PLUG MY MUSIC ANY TIME I can. I know it's commercialism at its lowest form . . . Bite me, again. It's beginning to feel good.

ROLL ME UP AND SMOKE ME WHEN I DIE

Roll me up and smoke me when I die
And if anyone don't like it, just look 'em in the eye
I didn't come here, and I ain't leavin'
So don't sit around and cry
Just roll me up and smoke me when I die.

You won't see no sad and teary eyes
When I get my wings, and it's my time to fly
Just call my friends and tell them

There's a party, come on by
So just roll me up and smoke me when I die.

Roll me up and smoke me when I die
And if anyone don't like it, just look 'em in the eye
I didn't come here, and I ain't leavin'
So don't sit around and cry
Just roll me up and smoke me when I die.

Well take me out and build a roaring fire
And roll me in the flames for 'bout an hour
And then pull me out and twist me up
And point me towards the sky
And roll me up and smoke me when I die.

Roll me up and smoke me when I die
And if anyone don't like it, just look 'em in the eye
I didn't come here, and I ain't leavin'
So don't sit around and cry
Just roll me up and smoke me when I die.

I didn't come here, and I ain't leavin'
So don't sit around and cry
Just roll me up and smoke me when I die.

And I say unto any man or woman, let your soul stand cool and collected before a million universes.

—Walt Whitman

LITTLE OLD FASHIONED KARMA

Just a little old fashioned karma coming down
A little old fashioned justice going round
It really ain't hard to understand
If you wanna dance you gotta pay the band
Just a little old fashioned karma coming down
Coming down
Coming down

Just a little old fashioned karma coming down
It really ain't hard to understand
If you wanna dance you gotta pay the band
Just a little old fashioned karma coming down

GOD

If we are children of God, then we must be gods too. Very small children must be God also. We were made in His image, duh. Why don't we know it and act like it? I don't know, maybe we do know and are afraid to accept the responsibility. If we admit that we are children of God, we can go a long way toward fixing what's wrong. Maybe that is our reason to be here, end of story.

TURN OUT THE LIGHTS

Turn out the lights the party's over
They say that all good things must end

Call it a night
The party's over
And tomorrow starts the whole damn thing again

Once I had a love undying
Didn't keep it wasn't trying
Life for me was just one party then another
Broke her heart so many times had to have my party wine
Then one night she said sweetheart
The party's over
Turn out the lights the party's over
They say that all good things must end
Call it a night the party's over
And tomorrow starts the whole damn thing
Again

JAMEY JOHNSON CAME BY TODAY. HE SAID HE WAS CAMPING OUT now, way out in the woods where he could be alone. You get that way sometimes. He is trying to write songs, so I told him what Roger Miller said: "Sometimes the well goes dry, and you need to stop and let it fill up again." With me, writing songs is not a choice. It's like labor pains, and they have to get out. It doesn't matter whether they are great ideas or just mind-farts, they just have to get out.

APRIL 5, 1:30 P.M.
   We are headed to Odessa, Texas, for a show tonight.

APRIL 6, 12:20 A.M.

Odessa was a really great crowd. Everyone came to have a good time, and I think they did.

We are now on our way to Oklahoma.

I THOUGHT ABOUT YOU, LORD

I thought about trees
And how much I'd like to climb one
I thought about friends
And how rare it is to find one

And I thought about you
The most gentle, sweet and kind one
I thought about you, Lord
I thought about you

There's breaking news on CNN, I'll be right back . . .

Okay, so it turns out there was an airplane that crashed into a bunch of houses. Nobody died, so that's a good thing.

APRIL 6

I went for a bike ride. It's kind of cool outside in Concho, Oklahoma—not bad, it could be worse, but I am glad we are playing inside tonight. We are playing a casino. Lana and her friend just went in to play the slots. I used to love to do that, even though I never won. They have to pay the light bills, I know, but no more with my money. Cold weather is much harder on the fans than the band. We have lights, heaters, etc., but the fans are right out there in it.

The Red Rocks Amphitheater is a good example of a perfect venue: the sound is great, and it's a beautiful location. The altitude is a little tough to sing in, but after a while you adjust to it.

Now I have ACL Live at the Moody Theater in Austin to play in too. The sound there is amazing, and even the farthest seat is up close. For me, Austin, Texas, is hard to beat. I love hot, dry weather, and being raised in Abbott, Texas, where it can really get hot, I survive pretty well. In Austin and the Hill Country. I'm like a lizard. Bring it on!

I'm trying to stay in warm country as much as I can, like Texas, Oklahoma, and Louisiana, but Texas mostly. At some point I'll work closer to home in Austin, San Antonio, Dallas, and Fort Worth. We are doing the Fourth of July picnic at Billy Bob's in Fort Worth this year, and that should be a blast. The whole family will be there. It will be me, Lukas, Micah, Amy, Paula, and many more. There will be three stages inside and out. I hope it's hot!

I might decide to do a yearlong tour overseas. Amsterdam, London, Paris, Rome, Amsterdam, Belfast, and then maybe Amsterdam again. I love Europe, because the fans are fantastic. Amsterdam is heaven. I wish Amsterdam was warmer country.

HEAVEN OR HELL

Sometimes it's heaven
Sometimes it's hell
And sometimes I don't even know
Sometimes I take it as far as I can
And sometimes I don't even go
My front tracks are headed for a cold-water well
My back tracks are covered with snow
Sometimes it's heaven
And sometimes it's hell
And sometimes I don't even know

Heaven ain't walking on a street paved with gold
And hell ain't no mountain of fire
Heaven is lying in my sweet baby's arms
And hell is when baby ain't there
My front tracks are headed for a cold-water well
And my back tracks are covered with snow
Sometimes it's heaven and sometimes it's hell
And sometimes I don't even know

EXERCISE

Work out, work out, and work out. If saying it again would convince you, I would gladly say it again . . . *Work out!* Exercise, exercise, exercise, but don't overdo it.

If you pull a muscle, rest until you heal, then work out some more. It's the best thing you can do for your sanity, not to mention your body. Exercise is good medicine, so follow your body—it won't lie. Do what it says. If it says move, then move. If it says rest, then rest. It's not that hard; your body does not lie, it does not *know how to* lie. If it hurts, it complains; if it feels good, it says, "Give me more of *this*."

I SEEM TO HAVE BEEN ADDICTED TO SOMETHING MOST OF MY LIFE. I started out smoking cigarettes. It bears repeating that I was about six when I started smoking cedar bark and grapevine, and rolling up Bull Durham. I was trading a dozen eggs for a pack of Camels. Then I ran into beer and whiskey, pills, and then pot. By then I was twenty-five years old and my lungs were killing me. Then came Percodan and painkillers of all kinds, just to keep my lungs from hurting. So then I said to myself, "Hey, you're not getting high on cigarettes, and they killed half your family." They just hurt my lungs. I would take a drag off a cigarette and my lungs would kill me. So I started quitting everything. No more cigarettes at all. I started running again and getting back in shape. I took my cigarettes and threw them away. I rolled up twenty joints and put them in the cigarette package, and every time I wanted a cigarette, I smoked a hit or two off a joint instead. One joint would last all day and it worked for me. Now I use a vaporizer, because it is easier on a singer's lungs.

APRIL 9
   Oxford, Mississippi, is nice. We are having great weather, so I had a good bike ride today. It's 7:56 P.M., and almost showtime.

APRIL 12

Here we are in Illinois now. I spent the last several hours
in a bus garage. Some kind of wheel problem. Tony and Gator
got it fixed, and now we are sitting in a parking lot somewhere.
Somebody on TV is talking about Rick Santorum dropping
out of the presidential race. It's a crazy time politically. All
the Republicans are chopping each other up pretty hard.
Romney is going be the guy, so it's an Obama and Romney
shoot-out.

"Shoot low, Shirley, she's riding a Shetland."

I like Obama a lot. I met him first when he was a senator from
Chicago. He came to the bus and we became friends. I am also a
Hillary Clinton fan, so when they both ran for president, I knew
I couldn't lose. Either way we'd win. As it turned out, Obama
couldn't do everything he wanted to, but Hillary probably couldn't
have either.

I think that once you become president, the first thing
you realize is that you can't do shit. I envision them getting
the new president in a little round room and letting him know
that he has no power and will do what he is told, just like Bill
Hicks said, years ago. Or like my old friend B. C. Cooper
used to say, "The town's fixed, the mayor is queer, turn the
crank!"

It's kind of like Texas, where no one is in control. Texas has
the right to secede from the union, and one day it might. Texas has
a lot of oil, wind, sun, and plenty of other natural resources, so it
would do okay, I think, but I don't want Texas to secede from the

union. *Texas can help keep America moving forward. Texas farm-ers could help make America become more energy independent by growing our fuel and developing more of our alternative energy. We could run the world on hot air alone.*

Texas is really better than we say it is. Oh, I could go on and on, but I won't. I wrote a song about Texas . . . I called it "Texas."

TEXAS

Listen to my song and if you want to sing along
It's about where I belong: Texas
Sometimes far into the night
And until the morning light
I pray with all my might to be in Texas
It's the only place for me
It's where I want to be
Where my spirit can be free: Texas.

Lord, look what time it is. I better go to bed so I can get up again.

COULD BE EVERY DAY

We got Wild Bill Elliott on the TV in the back of the bus, Randi Rhodes and Mike Malloy on SiriusXM Radio, and Emmylou up front on the other station. Life is good. Rick Santorum is talking now on the radio about his sweater vest. He has a sweater vest, I have a bandanna. Cool.

Speaking of Mike Malloy, I was listening to him one night and he said, "Come on back, Jesus, and get rid of some of these bastards!" It made me think to write this song:

COME ON BACK JESUS

Come on back Jesus (come on back Jesus)
Come on back Jesus
And pick up John Wayne on the way
The world's done gone crazy,
And it seems to get worse every day
So come on back Jesus,
And pick up John Wayne on the way

Time to take off the glove
They just don't respect peace anymore
But if we have old John Wayne
We know he can swing from the floor
While he kicks their butt
We'll just stand there and watch him and pray

So come on back Jesus,
And pick up John Wayne on the way

Come on back Jesus (come on back Jesus)
Come on back Jesus

And pick up John Wayne on the way
The world's gettin' crazy,
And it seems to get worse every day
So come on back Jesus,
And pick up John Wayne on the way

It's getting real hairy
If only old duke man was here
He'd call me old bastard
From out past the atmosphere
Lord the news looked so scary
When I glanced at the paper today
So come on back Jesus,
And pick up John Wayne on the way

Come on back Jesus (come on back Jesus)
Come on back Jesus
And pick up John Wayne on the way
The world's gettin' crazy,
And it seems to get worse every day
So come on back Jesus,
And pick up John Wayne on the way
Come on back Jesus, come on back Jesus
Come on back Jesus
And pick up John Wayne on the way

WHAT DO YOU CALL A GUITAR PLAYER WITHOUT A GIRLFRIEND?
Homeless. One of the main reasons I played guitar was because the

girls liked guitar players, and I liked girls. I had a fan club when I was in high school, so you see why I'm so conceited. Wait, I said that already. Seriously, I'm really not conceited at all. If you don't believe I'm good, just ask me . . . just kidding.

HERO

Where is our hero tonight
The bars are all booming and he's nowhere in sight
Wherever he is Lord I hope he's alright
Where is our hero tonight

He used to be king of the bars
He's opened and closed 'em from Waco to Mars
Now he sings in the street and he sleeps in his car
But he used to be king of the bars
Where is our hero tonight
He left here at midnight he was high as a kite
Wherever he is Lord we hope he's alright
Where is our hero tonight

And where is our hero today
Can we just tag along we'll stay out of his way
Does he still write the sad songs
And can he still play
Where is our hero today

. . .

I love Rachel Maddow. She is on TV now with Mayor Antonio Villaraigosa. They are taking about same-sex marriage and Obama, etc. It's pretty cool, and a good MSNBC program. Okay, now what? Oh, Rachel is on Leno tonight. I'll have to watch her again.

PHASES AND STAGES/WASHING THE DISHES

Phases and stages circles and cycles and scenes that we've all seen before
Let me tell you some more

Washing the dishes scrubbing the floors
Caring for someone who don't care anymore
Learning to hate all the things that she once loved to do
Like washing his shirts and never complaining except of red stains on the collars
Ironin' and cryin' cryin' and ironin' caring for someone who don't care anymore
Someday she'll just walk away

Phases and stages circles and cycles scenes that we've all seen before
Let me tell you some more

SOMEBODY PICK UP MY PIECES

Somebody pick up my pieces
I'm scattered everywhere
And put me back together
And put me way over there
Take me out of contention
I surrender my crown
So somebody pick up my pieces
It's just me comin' down

Well, I sure thought I had her
Lord, I know she had me
What I thought was heaven
Is just falling debris
Well, I may not be crazy
But I got one hell of a start
Somebody pick up my pieces
I think I'm fallin' apart

Don't follow my footsteps
Step over my trail
The road is too narrow
And your footing could fail
And the fall to the bottom
Could tear you apart
And they'll be pickin' up pieces
Of you and your heart

Don't follow my footsteps
Step over my trail

The road is too narrow
And your footing could fail
And the fall to the bottom
Could tear you apart
And they'll be pickin' up pieces
Of you and your heart
And they'll be pickin' up pieces
Of you and your heart

SUNDAY, APRIL 15

We are somewhere on the road right now, headed to Spring-
field, Missouri, and listening to Thom Hartmann on SiriusXM
Radio. I had a job washing dishes at a restaurant in Springfield,
back before I moved to Nashville. My wife, Martha, was working
there also. In Springfield, the Ozark Jubilee *was a very popular*
country music show. That's where I became friends with Shirley
Collie, Red Foley, Grady Martin, and Billy Walker, who moved
to Nashville. Billy Walker let me and Martha and Lana come stay
with him until we could find a place to live. He was a great friend,
and he was the first guy to record "Funny How Time Slips Away."

Shameless plug alert! Speaking of SiriusXM Radio, did I mention
that I have my own channel called Willie's Roadhouse (XM chan-
nel 56 and Sirius channel 64), where I get to play all the music
from my heroes from the past and present?

On Willie's Roadhouse you can hear the greatest entertain-
ers in country music, coming to you every week from Nashville's
Grand Ole Opry, with people like Little Jimmy Dickens and Bill
Anderson. Little Jimmy Dickens is ninety-one years old. He says,

Me in the studio

"When I drop something now, I bend over and look around to see if there's anything else I can do while I'm down there!"

One time me and Bill Anderson were flying from Nashville to San Antonio. We were talking about entertaining in Texas. Bill said, "Will, I just can't seem to do that well down here in Texas." I said, "Well, hell, Bill, they drink beer louder than you sing!"

Jeannie Seely and Connie Smith are great singers and good friends of mine. I'm glad to have them singing on the Roadhouse. One of the main purposes for me having my channel was to be able to help touring artists like Amber Digby, Tony Booth, Johnny Bush, Ray Price, Jamey Johnson, Jerry Jeff Walker, Jody Nix, Tommy Alverson, Asleep at the Wheel, Lukas Nelson, Paula

Nelson, Amy Nelson (I should have called it the Nepotism Channel), and Leona Williams.

I get to fine-tune the channel with my producer Jeremy Tepper, and Dallas Wayne does a great job spinning the country hits from Austin. It's a work in progress, and hopefully will stay that way.

MY NEW ALBUM *HEROES* IS NO. 15 ON THE TOP 100 ALBUMS, AND No. 4 on the country charts in the U.S.! Buddy Cannon and I picked the tunes and, as I said, brought in some great pickers from Nashville to my studio in Austin, where we joined Lukas and Micah and cut the tracks. We also cut some tracks in L.A. with Kris Kristofferson, Lukas, and Micah. I love working with Buddy because he knows all the best pickers to call. He's also a great writer and one of the best producers ever. He's not a bad guitar player and singer either.

Micah, Buddy Cannon, Kris Kristofferson,
me, and Butch Carr

My friend Snoop Dogg was gracious enough to sing with me on my new album too. We teamed up on "Roll Me Up" with Kris, Micah, Jamey, and Lukas. Thanks, Snoop!

I had the help of a lot of my heroes on *Heroes*: Sheryl Crow (one of my favorite singers), Ray Price, and Merle Haggard, another great singer and writer. Merle has written some of the best songs ever, like "Today I Started Loving You Again," "Ramblin' Fever," "Mama Tried," "Silver Wings," and so many more. We still pick together any time we can.

Merle, Ray Price, and I did a CD called *The Last of the Breed*. We all sang on the Cindy Walker CD too. I hope we can do more again soon.

FUNNY HOW TIME SLIPS AWAY

Well, hello there
My, it's been a long, long time
How am I doing?
Oh, I guess that I'm doing fine
It's been so long now,
But it seems now, that it was only yesterday
Gee, ain't it funny, how time slips away.

How's your new love?
I hope that he's doin' fine
I heard you told him,
That you'd love him till the end of time

Now, that's the same thing that you told me
Seems like just the other day
Gee, ain't it funny, how time slips away.

I gotta go now
I guess I'll see you around
Don't know when though
Never know, when I'll be back in town
But remember, what I tell you
In time you're gonna pay
And it's surprising, how time slips away . . .

YESTERDAY'S WINE

Miracles appear
In the strangest of places
Fancy meeting you here
The last time I saw you
Was just out of Houston
Sit down let me buy you a beer
Your presence is welcome
With me and my friend here
This is a hangout of mine
We come here quite often
And listen to music
Partaking of yesterday's wine
Yesterday's wine
I'm yesterday's wine

Aging with time
Like yesterday's wine
Yesterday's wine
We're yesterday's wine
Aging with time
Like yesterday's wine

You give the appearance
Of one widely traveled
I'll bet you've seen
Things in your time
So sit down beside me
And tell me your story
If you think
You'll like yesterday's wine
Yesterday's wine
We're yesterday's wine
Aging with time
Like yesterday's wine

Yesterday's wine
We're yesterday's wine
Aging with time
Like yesterday's wine

I GOTTA GET DRUNK

Well, I gotta get drunk and I sure do dread it
Cuz I know just what I'm gonna do
I'll start to spend my money callin' everybody honey
And I'll wind up singin' the blues
I'll spend my whole paycheck on some old wreck
And brother I can name you a few
Well, I gotta get drunk and I sure do dread it
Cuz I know just what I'm gonna do

Well, I gotta get drunk, I can't stay sober
There's a lot of good people in town
Who like to see me holler, see me spend my dollar
And I wouldn't dream of lettin' 'em down
There's a lot of doctors that tell me
That I'd better start slowin' it down
But there's more old drunks than there are old doctors
So I guess we'd better have another round

April 15, 1:30 p.m.

    I am playing Wii golf on the bus with David, and there is a storm coming. I'm glad the show is inside tonight. It's one thirty p.m., and so far so good, but it looks like we are still in the path of the bad weather. It's amazing the number of bad storms we are having. We are definitely in a changing world. I've said before that the Earth is a living entity, and it takes care of itself. The Bible says, "If thy right eye offend thee pluck it out." It is a huge tiger with a thorn in its paw. Earth will take out the thorn and everything else in its way. Earth is always healing itself, mainly because we are always harming it in some way. The water and air on Earth are being adversely affected by our bad habits. We are fucking up our home . . . damn, are we dumb.

2:25 P.M.

Looking out the window of the bus, David says we have fifteen minutes before the storm hits. The weather is still bad. There have been one hundred tornadoes this week, and five people so far didn't make it to the next day. One tornado destroyed a town and one hundred people have been displaced, from Texas to Wisconsin. Otha Lee Boyd and I were in the middle of a tornado one time. It killed one hundred sixty people. I have the utmost respect for tornadoes. If I were a music fan in this area, and I asked myself where I wanted to be on a night like this, my answer would be home. I wouldn't blame them at all if that's what they decided. I think the worst is over, though. I hope so. But we are all in this sinking ship together.

Ahoy, matey!

Whew, no problem, we dodged another bullet! Thank you very much, weatherman or weatherwoman, whichever. You who do weather.

Bill Cosby is on TV now. He is a great guy and a great friend. One time he asked, "What do you need?" when I needed millions, and I knew he was serious. Thanks, Bill!

I haven't quite figured out this walking-on-water stuff. I had a great day of golf today with all the gang. We didn't play that well, but we had fun and got some fresh air. I needed to get off the bus for a while.

I woke up one night about two in the morning, in Ridgetop, Tennessee. I was reading in the paper where some guy killed his girlfriend, so I wrote:

I JUST CAN'T LET YOU SAY GOODBYE

I had not planned on seeing you
I was afraid of what I'd do
But pride is strong and here am I
And I just can't let you say goodbye

Please have no fear you're in no harm
As long as you're here in my arms
But you can't leave so please don't try
I just can't let you say goodbye
What force behind your evil mind
Can make your lips speak so unkind
To one who loves as much as I
I just can't let you say goodbye
The flesh around your throat is pale
Indented by my fingernails

Please don't scream and please don't cry
I just can't let you say goodbye

Your voice is still it speaks no more
You'll never hurt me anymore
Death is a friend to love and I
'Cause now you'll never say goodbye

There was a guy in the Junction Bar in San Antonio who loved that song. He would come walking toward the bandstand choking himself, with his hands around his throat, which is how I knew that he wanted me to sing that song.

TUESDAY, APRIL 17

We play St. Louis tonight, then on to Austin. I'm ready to see
my ponies.

I'm back in the cabin, and there's another great sunset. When
Waylon Jennings, Larry Trader, and I first came up here, I knew
I had found a spot. This is it, and it don't get no better than this,
end of story.

There is still a little chill in the air. I thought I'd hit the
pool . . . wrong. I'm real wimpy about cold water. Hot water,
that's okay. I like hot water. I get myself in it all the time.

A GUY WENT TO THE DOCTOR FOR A CHECKUP. THE DOCTOR SAID, "Well, first of all, sir, you'll have to stop masturbating." The guy said, "Why?" The doctor said, "So I can examine you!"

• • •

This is a good time for a hit and a hot coffee. I call it hillbilly heroin.

APRIL 18

Dick Clark passed away today from a heart attack. He was really one of the good guys and brought a lot of great music together. He was just eighty-two years old. He did American Bandstand *starting back around 1956. He created the show, and they called him America's oldest teenager.*

When I was six years old, maybe before, I was writing poems about things like good love, bad love, and broken hearts before I was old enough to know about those things. I do believe in reincarnation and that I came back to write things down—I just started early. I wrote poems until I learned to play guitar; then I started writing songs, and I have never stopped. I had some times when I wrote more. But like Roger Miller said, sometimes the well goes dry and you have to wait till the well fills up again. Roger was great. Mel Tillis said, "Roger could rhyme shit and claw hammer," and I think he could.

SISTER BOBBIE

Our education was very important to Mama Nelson. It was when Willie was in first grade that his teacher, Miss Dianne, told her of Willie's very noticeable writing ability. He had written a poem that had impressed the teacher a lot. Mama was so proud. She could not wait to tell me. It was at this young age that Willie started writing, first poems and then songs. We would perform his new compositions for the congregation at revival church meetings. It is obvious today that his writing has continued and we are still performing his compositions. Where we first performed in church, then school, we joined others to play music, from his polka band to our first swing band—with our father and my husband, who formed our first honky-tonk band. We were making music, building a fan base, having a lot of fun and enjoyment, and learning more music and playing it better.

Where were we? Oh yes, we are going to Lufkin, Texas.

THURSDAY, APRIL 19

Lufkin went great, and we had a really great crowd. We had good weather, and it was an outside show, so perfect.

4/20, AUSTIN, TEXAS

Today is my statue day, at the corner of Lavaca Street and Willie Nelson Boulevard, and Johnny Cash's birthday bash in Austin at the W Hotel, in Austin City Limits Live at the Moody Theater. Did I mention the sculpture is on Willie Nelson Boulevard? The sculptor is a man named Clete Shields from Philadelphia, Pennsylvania. They are presenting the statue today on 4/20 at 4:20. It will be a good day. My son Micah is with me. He will play with me at the Cash birthday show and at the statue presenta-

*tion. Then maybe he will paint a picture of it all. He is such a great
artist, and I can't draw a circle. It just don't figure. But I can draw
a crowd, I guess, and so hopefully they will be there for me today.*

CHRIS ETHRIDGE

Chris Ethridge died today, April 23, 2012, from complications with
cancer. Chris played bass in my band. He was a great musician and
a good friend. Chris played bass with me when Bee took a job with
Waylon. Then Bee came back and we had two bass players, and at
one time we had two bass players and two drummers. Everything
was great until we all got on different drugs; then it sounded a lot
like a cluster fuck and a catfight going on at the same time, but we
had fun. Anyway, Chris was sixty-five years old. He will be missed.

ONE STEP BEYOND

*I'm just one step before losing you
and I'm just one step ahead of the blues
and I know that there's been pain and misery
long before this old world ever heard of me
It will hurt me so much to see you go
But we'll just add one more heartache to the score
And though I still love you as before
I'm just one step beyond caring anymore*

*I guess that you're surprised that I could feel this way
after staying home and waiting night and day*

for someone who cared so much for me
you'd come home just long enough to laugh at me
I don't know just when my feelings changed
I just know I could never feel the same
and though I still love you as before
I'm just one step beyond caring anymore

WE HAD A GOOD LAUGH TODAY TALKING ABOUT MY STATUE WITH Michael Hall from *Texas Monthly.* He was here today doing a piece on me and Trigger. Trigger loved it.

I AM THINKING I WANT TO PUT "YESTERDAY'S WINE" BACK IN MY show. I just heard it on my SiriusXM channel, performed by George Jones and Waylon Jennings. Pretty cool.

THERE'S A NEW MOVIE I'M IN, CALLED *WHEN ANGELS SING.* ALL THE actors did a great job, I thought. It will be coming out . . . duh, around Christmas! I like it because it's a real family movie. I think we need more family movies. I may need to work on scoring the music for it, and that will be easy, but I guess I'm looking old. Did I mention that I was in it? Oh well.

THERE SEEMS TO BE A WAR ON WOMEN, AT LEAST IN THE MEDIA. WE won't win that one . . . period. We can't let our mockingbird mouths overload our hummingbird asses.

THE ART OF FARTING

MAY 2012

We are on a break and flying back to Maui. It looks like the ocean and the clouds are getting closer. I hope we're landing. They say landing an airplane is like a controlled crash. I wish they wouldn't say shit like that.

We are about three hours out now. Annie has her face covered because there's a little kid coughing openly, really bad, and spreading her germs everywhere. So I just farted and sent it her way. That should kill all the germs on the plane. My farts have been known to kill johnsongrass six feet high. My grandmother slapped a fart out of me one time that whistled like a freight train. It scared both of us really bad. She never hit me again.

That little girl doesn't even know to say thank you, but I hope someday she might be able to do the same for somebody else. It's okay, little girl, I'm a pretty nice guy once you get to know me, and if you ever need any more emergency medical help just send me your home address, and I will fart in your general direction. You're welcome.

MAY 6

I'm on the bus drinking buttermilk—well, actually, it's an organic, lactose-free kefir that Annie gets for me to drink, because it's healthier. I have plenty of lactose and I don't know if I need what I got, so it's probably good. I've never lacked in lactose as far as I know. Lactose could be one of those things that you don't know you have too much of until you die. It happens I'm sure.

Oh well, here goes nothing. It's really good, but I tried to get Steve Gilchrist, another poker buddy, to taste it. He almost threw it up. Apparently he's not a kefir guy.

We played poker two days straight after my show at the Backyard, which was great if I do say so myself. It was a sold-out crowd. Jamey Johnson, Paula Nelson, and Amy Nelson played too. Mudslide has been here for a few days helping out. My seventy-ninth birthday is coming up. I hope to get all the kids over for a little party. Annie loves it when all the family is there and she can feed them all, so I'm guessing it will happen.

WHAT DO YOU GET WHEN YOU CROSS A ROOSTER WITH ANOTHER rooster? A very cross rooster!

Speaking of chickens . . . one time I went over to Bee Spears's house after he had just gotten back from the feed store with some corn for the chickens in his backyard. He dropped the corn and it spilled all over the bedroom floor. We decided that the best way to clean it up was to bring the chickens into the bedroom.

We did and they ate all the corn. It was a brilliant idea. Then we noticed that one chicken would take a bite of corn and then raise her right leg. She did it every time. So when Bee's wife came home, she wanted to know what was going on.

Bee told her we had been training chickens. He pointed at the one hen and said, "Watch this." She said, "Okay," so he waited till the one chicken ate a kernel of corn. Then Bee said, "Okay, honey, raise your right leg," and of course the chicken did! We laughed a lot.

• • •

I WANT TO BRING UP MY FAVORITE GUITAR PLAYER AGAIN. DJANGO Reinhardt is the best, period. I play "Nuages" and a couple more Django songs every show. I heard one of the Little Willies—Norah Jones's band—said I played "like Django with one finger." That's about the nicest thing anyone has ever said about my playing, because as we all know Django only had two fingers because of the fire and was still the best guitar player that ever lived. Just to think for a minute that I might be half as good as Django makes my head a little bigger, so thank you.

Django

Norah is a sweetheart and a great musician; I love singing with her. Her band the Little Willies is really great. How do you think that makes me feel? I was and always will be floored. Thanks, Norah. I love you.

A GUY WAS IN A COMA FOR YEARS. HE WOKE UP ONE DAY AND SMELLED his favorite food, chocolate cookies. He crawled out of bed and all the way down the hall to the kitchen. When he got there, sure enough, there they were. He put his hand up to reach one, and his wife slapped him on the hand and said, "No, honey, those are for the funeral!"

PERMANENTLY LONELY

Don't be concerned it's time I learned
That those who play with fire get burned
But I'll be all right in a little while
But you'll be permanently lonely

Don't be too quick to pity me
Don't salve my heart with sympathy
'Cause I'll be all right in a little while
But you'll be permanently lonely

The world looks on with wonder and pity at your kind
'Cause it knows that the future is not very pretty for your kind

For your kind will always be running and wondering
What's happened to hearts that you've broken and left all alone
But we'll be all right in a little while
But you'll be permanently lonely
Running . . . Lonely . . .

FREDDY POWERS WILL BE COMING OUT TO SEE ME TOMORROW. HE has been a little under the weather. He is a good friend and one of the best rhythm players there ever was. He played the Django stuff, and jazz, as good as anybody, and it will be good to see him. He is also a great songwriter. He wrote songs like "A Friend in California" and "I Always Get Lucky with You." He traveled with Merle Haggard's band a lot, and Merle sang many Freddy Powers songs.

I can't see
I can't pee
I can't chew
I can't screw
If the golden years are here at last
Then the golden years can kiss my ass
—WORDS OF WISDOM FROM RAY PRICE

POODIE USED TO SAY, "IT'S OKAY TO STEP ON YOUR DICK, JUST DON'T stand on it," and "A farting horse never tires."

. . .

OKAY, WHERE WERE WE? OH YES, HERE WE ARE. ALWAYS BE WHERE you are, I say, and it's always now, and that's about it. The full significance of the moment is being realized now, thank you, let's move on.

I THINK WE ARE GETTING CLOSER TO THE END OF MAJOR WARS BE-cause they cost too much. I think it will get broken into several small wars all over the world and the reason will be *for survival*. Food and water will become hard to get. If they—"they" being anybody—run out of food and water they will come after yours out of desperation. Think about it: if your kids are hungry, thirsty, and sick, you will do anything to save them, anything.

That's when the shit will hit the fan and it will be everybody for themselves, like a dog-eat-dog, only-the-strong-survive scenario. It won't be pretty. We will be our brother's keeper, and we will try to keep some sense of sanity alive and care for whomever. If they need it and we got it, we share as long as it lasts. More will be provided, and we will need to take a lot of lemons and make a shitload of lemonade. More will be provided, and we will eventu-ally work our way back to prosperity. All races and religions will come together, knowing it's the only way to survive. We all eat, sleep, laugh, cry, live, and die the same. We will find that it will be much easier and cheaper to stick together, and it will be God's way of bringing peace on earth. When they throw a war and no one shows up, it will serve as a new beginning of peace on earth. Amen.

• • •

My son Micah has been busy with his art and music for a while now. He does something called Cymatics, where he makes art with music, water, and vibration, and then he projects it all on a wall or screen. It's way beyond me, but he seems to have a pretty strong following. I like that he is so diverse in his art, and that he and Lukas like all kinds of music. Micah just made a live painting during one of Lukas's performances, which Annie and I bought. It came out beautiful. We have learned now that in order to actually get to keep what he creates, we have to claim it before he paints it, or someone else will outbid us for it!

I'm learning to play with some of the online media stuff like YouTube so that I can see his work—and the rest of the kids' stuff too.

Lukas is in Canada right now on tour. He is getting to be a chip off the old block, as they say, working even more dates than me every year. He just got back from Haiti, where he had a guitar camp for kids that Sean Penn had set up. Sean's another good guy who puts his money where his mouth is. Anyway, it was a really great experience for him, and he wrote a song about Haiti while he was there, so I guess you'll be hearing that soon, too.

ANNIE NELSON

Both of our boys started at the Montessori School of Maui at the age of two. I loved the idea that they would have the opportunity to "learn how to learn" instead of learning the answers to tests. We were lucky that we could afford to give them a good education, because that was something I felt no one could ever take from them. They thrived in the Montessori setting, so I made sure we had a good school in Austin as well, mostly because the Montessori pedagogy was clear that lessons and life could happen anywhere, so travel wasn't a big deal, and travel was our "normal." I have a magnet on my refrigerator that says THE ONLY NORMAL PEOPLE ARE THE ONES YOU DON'T REALLY KNOW. When the boys were little, they would hear comments that our life wasn't "normal," and the lesson that there really is no normal was the most important one to teach them.

Lukas was five weeks old before anyone outside of our family got a peek at him. It was at the Grammy Awards show, and my husband was receiving a Lifetime Achievement Award from the Recording Academy. I remember pulling up in the bus, and just before we were ready to step out of the bus Mark Rothbaum (Willie's manager) started teasing me by bringing up all the money we were offered, and turned down, for photos of Lukas. We had refused, so when we stepped out, with Lukas in his onesie tuxedo, Willie and me dressed to the nines, and the cameras clicking away, Mark started going on about how I had just blown Lukas's college fund. Mark has to have a good sense of humor to keep up, and he really is one of the funniest. In any case, we walked down the red carpet (yuck!) and got to the end, where Rick Dees was to interview Willie. Rick asked Willie a few questions, which I cannot remember because the red carpet is terrifying to me, but then he put the microphone in Lukas's face and said, "Lukas, what do you think about your daddy getting this award?" And as if on cue, Lukas yawned like he was bored as could be, which cracked everyone up and made the papers. Maybe Lukas just knew what was coming and that his life would be so similar to his father's (ergo the yawn)...who knows?

Then came Micah...way too quickly! Our boys are exactly sixteen months apart in age, to the day! Lukas was born December 25, and Micah was born April 25, a few days before his father's birthday on the thirtieth. Our boys are each other's yin and yang, and therefore balance each other's personalities well. They grew up like twins and are best friends to this day. Micah too is an amazing musician. He hears music in ways that are just as abstract as the ways he sees life when he paints or draws. I love all kinds of music, and both boys heard every type of music we could find from my collection as well as their father's. Micah can take music and mix it with art, projection, water, and vibration to create even more art. It's amazing if I do say so myself. My father nicknamed Micah

"MicahAngelo" because before he could walk, he was scribbling on anything he could find. He is an amazing artist, as witnessed by some of his paintings in this book, and I know I'm his mother, but I'm not the only one who thinks so, so I'm not just "being a mom" when I say it.

You know how your little child will draw pictures and you put them on your fridge? Well, the ones I got from Micah went in my "Mom book." I remember one Christmas when Micah was four years old and gave me a little drawing. It wasn't just a normal drawing; I got a perfect Santa in a sleigh, circling in the sky while presents, in perfect perspective, fell from the bag in the sleigh into the perfectly proportioned chimney of a perfectly proportioned home covered in snow. That's when I started my Mom book.

I highly recommend, if you have children, that you start your book as soon as your child is able to create. I have a lifetime of memorable gifts in my Mom book and wouldn't trade it for the world. We didn't spoil the boys with things. They spent their lives outside in nature, surfing, playing soccer, playing baseball, and discovering the world. They were never given cars or any kind of material junk, but they were spoiled with experiences that helped to create the citizens of the world that they are to this day, and their dad and I are very proud of the people they have become. I am proud of everyone in my family, on both my side and Willie's. But I am especially proud of how we have managed to blend three lovely families of amazing people (how could they not be with him as a father, right?), and how loving, kind, and sharing all of our kids are. You probably feel it when you see them all together onstage, but it is with the help of the ones not on-stage too, and they all get it. We are all very blessed.

For all of their lives our boys were not allowed to buy us gifts. If they wanted to give us something they made it. They took a great deal of joy in creating things, and it was always encouraged. Those are the things that fill my Mom book.

Both Lukas and Micah are very gifted with intellect, compassion, and a sense of art and music . . . and I'm sure they get it all from my side . . . just kidding . . . kind of.

I HEARD THAT LUKAS, MICAH, AND AMY ARE ALL GOING TO PLAY some shows together soon. Really love it when my family all makes music together.

SISTER BOBBIE IS MY ROCK. SHE HAS BEEN WITH ME SINCE, WELL, since I first started breathing on this planet. We both learned the language of music from our grandparents, who taught music. Bobbie can read and write music, and can decipher anything I throw at her. I love her attitude about life. She always sees the good in people, and that's what people see back in her. She is the best piano player for me. She rolls with whatever I throw at her, and it doesn't matter where I run off to in music, she is always there when I get back. She is beautiful. No one ever would guess her age; she just looks timeless, which is probably why she has all the boys, young and old, in her pocket whenever she hangs out.

She thinks I hung the moon; did I mention that?

Bobbie is also a great cook, and she loves to do it. She cooks for me all the time on the bus, and whenever I'm in Austin and Annie's not, my sister Bobbie feeds me and I love it. She makes the best biscuits, gravy, and eggs you will ever eat, and it's not just my opinion. Even when Annie is there, Bobbie's is our first choice whenever we can go there for breakfast.

Sister Bobbie with her
granddaughter, Ellee Fletcher

Sister Bobbie's son Freddy with
his daughter, Ellee, and wife, Lisa

Bobbie has had so much heartache in her life, yet somehow she just lives through it and shines as if her life has been a breeze. It hasn't, and that is real courage. Maybe it's the music that keeps us sane, because Sister Bobbie loves playing music as much as I do, and that's a lot!

She loves everyone, and she loves all my family (whew!). She is there with me most days and nights while I'm on tour, and I have never gotten tired of that fact. I love her company, and thank God, because touring is like living on a submarine together.

The best part about Bobbie is that she thinks I'm funny. I could hear her laugh all day long like good music. She is funny too. Just when I think no one gets a joke I've told, guess who laughs first? I couldn't do this without her.

SISTER BOBBIE

Our lives are all about music and love. Love and music, inseparable; nourishment for our body and our soul. I wake up with a song, and that's what Willie gives me: a life filled with love and music. That is what Willie gives to all those who listen.

I love you, my brother.

Your sister,
Bobbie

• • •

MY DAUGHTER AMY'S BAND FOLK UKE IS GREAT, TOO! THE BAND IS simply Amy and Cathy Guthrie (Arlo Guthrie's daughter) making beautiful music with great harmonies together. They sing some Depression-era music, but they are mostly known for songs that can't be played on regular radio—they are the best at that. They have great senses of humor, and it shows in their music.

AMY NELSON

I have two childhood memories that battle for the place of earliest. One is sucking my fingers and hiding behind a chair. The other is driving. I would sit on Dad's lap and steer the wheel. Together we would laugh as we bounced and wound up and down our driveway in Dripping Springs, Texas.

This is a snapshot of my dad. He was willing to put his life into the hands of a child in order to instill a sense of confidence and adventure in her. How cool is that?

When I was eight years old, he handed me a stack of mail and asked me to throw away everything that was not important.

I asked, "Should I show it to you before I throw it away?"

He said, "No, I trust you."

I love these memories because they are times in my life where I was treated as a capable, above-average kid, and for the most part, it made me act accordingly. I wonder now what I threw away.

"Never look directly into the sun," Mom warned me. Later, Dad would teach me to look directly into the sun just a little bit more each day, as is the practice of the sun gazers, who stare at the sun to achieve enlightenment.

I love that my dad looks at things in a different way, and I always appreciate the opportunity to do the same.

My dad is the hardest-working person I have ever known. Perhaps it's because he was a child laborer. He was staked out in a cotton field when he was a toddler so that his grandparents could work the fields and look after him at the same time. When he was old enough to pick the cotton, that's when he began working. And he didn't stop. Three-quarters of a century later, he is still working, and well into his retirement years.

"If you don't use it, you will lose it," I've heard him say numerous times. He was given an incredible voice and he uses it to heal the world. He's put in twenty-seven years with Farm Aid being a voice for farmers and nine years with the Animal Welfare Institute being a voice for horses. He has adopted seventy horses. He worked with Best Friends Animal Society to strengthen dogfighting laws in Georgia.

Aside from that, he has been uniting countless people with his music spanning the better part of the last century. He transcends boundaries, opens hearts, and unites people. He might be Jesus in disguise. Can you tell that I'm proud of him?

I wish everyone could be so fortunate as to have a dad like mine. That's part of why I don't mind sharing him with the world. In the spirit of sharing, here is a collective sample of Papa Willie wisdom:

Count your blessings. All we have is now, and it's always now. Music is the most powerful healing force, because it is the one thing that can instantaneously travel to your soul. Dynamic tension. Practice it daily. We get out of the world what we project onto the world. When the student is ready, the teacher will appear. Never underestimate your opponent. Spin around fifty times each direction at night before going to sleep to charge your chakras. If you're scared to do something, do it anyway. Do it because you are afraid. If there's anything worth doing, it's worth doing big. Either way, it takes the same amount of energy. If someone rips you off, consider it money well spent for a lesson that you will always remember. Find yourself another sucker. Horses are smarter than people. Don't pay attention to reviews: if you believe the good ones, then you will have to believe the bad ones. Whatever the problem, ask yourself, "Will it matter in a hundred years?" Physician, heal thyself. Do unto others as you would have them do unto you. Horses are smarter than people. Take my advice and do what you want to do. Don't be an asshole. Don't be an asshole. Don't be an asshole.

My daughter Paula is out in Colorado right now tearing up the towns with her band. She kicks ass! She is very proud of her little animal family. She has rescued donkeys, goats, dogs, cats, you name it! They are all family, so I have grandkiiids who have bigger beards than I do!

PAULA NELSON

As long as I can remember remembering, my father has been a calm and gentle hero to me. He'd sing a song called "Yeah Blue" to my sister Amy and me when we were very little. It was a sad song, but to hear him sing the melody was very comforting. He was on the road and we were in school, and it made it hard to spend a whole lot of time together growing up, but he was always only a phone call away. He's a great listener and has always supported his family in every way. He's my father, but he's also my friend.

My greatest joy is seeing all my kids onstage singing together. It's really hard to beat that DNA harmony sound. I'm really happy when they are all out singing individually, but knocked out when they are standing at the microphone right next to me, singing their hearts out together.

Amy, Paula, Mickey Raphael, and me

LANA NELSON

The things I do or have done are not the things I am. What I am is a daughter so proud of her father most days I can't discuss him without crying. He has always been there for me, never making me feel stupid for asking anything. I hope to somehow give back to him a tiny portion of what he has so freely given to each of us. It has been a lifelong goal to work with my dad in any capacity he may ever need, and I will be there until the end.

PAULA NELSON

I don't know any other family like our family. There are so many of us from different marriages, but yet we're all friends and very close. I believe it's because of him we are this way. He's a great and very wise teacher. I love him with all my heart and I am proud to be his daughter. He's my hero. He's my Papa Bear.

SUSIE NELSON

The eighties were traumatic for me, because my father was moving too fast. Today I'm okay with it. Faith requires me to hold a picture in my mind of what I wish to see happening. I know that my father represents that big picture. The art of the Holy Spirit, healing in song and guitar music, is obvious. His guitar instrumental "Matador" settles my spirit, and this daughter doesn't worry about her father out there anymore. Thank you, Dad, for your guitar, your music, and your songs.

LUKAS NELSON

I admire him, so I never want to disappoint him. Even in his absences throughout the years, the morals and values he has instilled in me just by my observing him have been firmly established. When he does give advice, I am always listening with alert ears, because he has had many years to spend with a peaceful mind, and therefore has gained immeasurable wisdom.

I feel blessed to have been born at this more mature point in his life as well. He seems to have a wise river to float down at his age, and it seems to be speaking to him and he seems to be listening. I can't know, obviously, everything that goes on in his head . . . but everything that comes out of it is rooted in love and experience. I will always strive to be the best man I know, and I am lucky because I have spent my whole life with him so far.

MICAH NELSON

My father and my mother both have always encouraged my brother and me to be our own people and stand on our own ideas as artists, but most of all, to be compassionate human beings with integrity and respect for others.

My father's sense of humor, his compassion, his love of family, his creativity—these are some of the most valuable things I inherited from him, and I am incredibly grateful to know him and be a part of his world. My ole man is by far my ultimate hero. I love you, Pap!

RAELYN NELSON

People always ask me what it's like to have P-dub as my grandpa. He's a loving, kind, generous, and funny grandpa. He's never been angry with me. His voice is always warm when we catch up on the phone, and he always has the most right thing to say in the moment. He has always been on the road, working and playing for his fans; he sure does love his fans. That's what we've always known: he was on the road, working, doing what he loves to do, and it's all for us anyway . . . and you.

ANNIE NELSON

I'm really lucky because I have a husband who is my friend as well as my love. Like all couples, we have had our differences in working out how to blend lives, families, and children. In our case we have a few families to blend, which isn't for the faint of heart—or sissies.

We are lucky to have an amazing and talented family. All of our kids are brilliant . . . yeah, I know, but honestly they were all blessed to have Willie as their father and must have chosen him for a reason. Maybe they were really good in their past lives and won the father lottery. Was he a "Disney dad"? Sure, but he always balanced it with reason if one of them went too far. A word from him, and they were easily steered back on track. He has a way of seeing life that is a gift to anyone who is lucky enough to spend time with him, so imagine his children's childhoods!

Anyway, that's about as much as I care to share, except to say that the most common question people ask me is, is it hard to be Willie's wife with all those women around, and always being interrupted? The answer is no. My husband knows where he lives, and I am grateful to everyone who hears the love in his voice through his music, and I understand . . . I love him too.

WHATEVER HAPPENED TO PEACE ON EARTH

There are so many things going on in the world
Babies dying, mothers crying
How much oil is one human life worth
And what happened to peace on earth

We believe everything they tell us
They are going to kill us so we gotta kill them first
But I remember the commandment thou shalt not kill

How much is that soldier's life worth
And what happened to peace on earth

And the bewildered herd's still believing
Everything they've been told from their birth
Hell they won't lie to me
Not on my own damn TV
How much is a liar's word worth
And what happened to peace on earth

Now you may not hear this on your radio
And not on your local TV
But if you have time and you're ever inclined
You can always hear it from me

And the bewildered herd's still believing
Everything we've been told from our birth
hell they won't lie to me,
Not on my own damn TV
But how much is a picker's life worth
And what happened to peace on earth

I KNOW I NEED TO END THIS BOOK BECAUSE I HAVE WRITTEN WAY TOO many words. And in the words of my old friend Larry Trader, "I'm tired of talking, the end." Time for the 2012 Olympics! I was just telling Annie that they have the Olympics and the Special Olympics, but they should have one for seniors only and just call it the LIMPics!

SUPERMAN

Too many pain pills
Too much pot
Trying to be something
That I'm not
Superman, Superman

Trying to do more than I can,
Got a little out of hand
I ain't Superman

Well I blew my throat
And I blew my tour
I wound up sippin' on
Soup du jour
I wasn't Superman
I wasn't Superman

Tryin' to do more than I can
Got a little out of hand
I ain't Superman

The doctor said son
It's a crying shame
But you ain't Clark Kent
And I ain't Lois Lane
You ain't Superman
You ain't Superman

Trying to do more than I can
Got a little out of hand
I ain't Superman

And when I die
Put it on my stone
God said sucker
Get your bad ass home
I wasn't Superman
I wasn't Superman

Trying to do more than I can
Got a little out of hand
I wasn't Superman

CREDITS

All illustrations by Micah Nelson

All photographs courtesy of Willie Nelson with the exception of:

Page 52: Budrock Prewitt
Page 64: Courtesy of Sony Music Entertainment
Page 65: Randie Laine K
Page 104: Nadav Benjamin, nadavbenjamin.com

Grateful acknowledgment is made for permission to reprint excerpts from the following:

"Roll Me Up and Smoke Me When I Die." Words and music by Buddy Cannon, Willie Nelson, John Colgin, Michael McQuerry, and Richard Alves. Copyright © 2011 Run Slow Music, Act Five Music, Warner-Tamerlane Publishing Corp., Colleywood Music, Cotton Valley Worldwide Publishing and Hard Labor Music. All rights for Run Slow Music administered by BMG Rights Management (US) LLC. Reprinted by permission of Hal Leonard Corporation. All rights for Act Five Music administered by Warner-Tamerlane Publishing Corp. Used by per-

CREDITS

CREDITS